The Coxswain's Manual

3rd edition

by
Joe Keeley

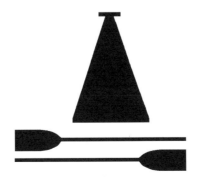

The Coxswain's Locker, Inc.
1998

ISBN 1-884287-01-8

© Copyright 1998, The Coxswain's Locker™, Inc.

All rights reserved.
No part of this book may be reproduced
in any form, by photostat, microfilm,
xerography, on the Internet or any
other means, or incorporated into any
information retrieval system, electronic or
mechanical, without the written permission
of the copyright owner.

All inquires should be addressed to:
The Coxswain's Locker™, Inc.
P.O. Box 1167
Washington, D.C. 20013
(703) 237-2696
www.coxing.com

PRINTED IN THE UNITED STATES OF AMERICA

Photographs used in this book were taken at the Dad Vail Regatta, Philadelphia, PA; Eastern Sprints, Worcester, MA; Mid-Atlantic H.S. Championships, Occuquan, VA; and elsewhere. The author would like to thank the assistance and consideration of the organizers and officials of these regattas.

Acknowledgments

This book would not have been possible without the patient and continuous assistance of several friends and coaches. They are as follows :

The Coaches
Stan Bergman
Larry Connell
Wiley Wakeman

The Models
Spencer Cutter
John Lynott
Chris Pedicone
Ed Pedicone
Sean Ryan

The Editor
Stacy Ogren Keeley

Chris Pedicone, John Lynott, Ed Pedicone, Spencer Cutter, and Sean Ryan

Author's Note

This book is based upon four years of coxing for the schoolboys program at Tabor Academy in Marion, Massachusetts and four more years for the heavyweight men's program at the University of Pennsylvania in Philadelphia. I currently row as a lightweight sculler in Washington, D.C. During my time spent coxing, I raced throughout the United States meeting and racing against numerous other coxswains and coaches. It is from these experiences that I drew upon to write the first and second editions of The Coxswain's Manual.

During my eight years of coxing, I had six coaches with a unique coaching style. Three of these coaches - Stan Bergman, Larry Connell, and Wiley Wakeman - felt that coxswains could be more than a sound piece and I am grateful to have coxed for them and for what they taught me. Since there was never a manual for coxswains, their instruction and guidance formed the basis for my knowledge and the first book. I also learned from my share of mistakes. My apologies to the referees and oarsmen who had to tolerate my lack of coxswain skills during my first few years.

This book is to be used with The Coxswain's Drill Card and The Coxswain's Video One and Two. The Coxswain's Locker, Inc. will continue to update its products as the sport changes. If you notice something in this book that you strongly like or dislike, please do not hesitate to write to us at the address below. We always appreciate your comments, both positive and negative.

It is my hope that you use this book to pursue whatever goals you may have - winning local club races, improving your performance in high school races, going to college and winning the national championships, competing as a master's coxswain, etc... And if you see a single named *A Coxswain No More*, don't criticize my technique - I'll never be a great rower, just a coxswain who grew too big.

Joe Keeley
November 1998

c/o The Coxswain's Locker, Inc.
P.O. Box 1167
Washington, DC 20013 USA
www.coxing.com

How to use this manual

This manual is primarily written for coxswains with up to three years of experience. It is also designed as a reference source for all coxswains. Some chapters can be skipped by coxswains with a year or two of experience who have already mastered the basics such as launching, steering, and landing a shell. Chapters One through Twelve cover a basic course of information for novice coxswains. Chapters Thirteen to Eighteen cover topics which may not arise until the end of a coxswain's first year.

Rowing terms are listed in **boldface** at their first usage. See Chapter Four, Terms for the definitions. Text printed in *italics* is spoken by you. I have used "he" throughout the book as a generic term, rather than alternate the pronouns "he" and "she."

All coxswains develop at varying rates. The estimated timelines for coxswains used in this book are for a typical freshman college coxswain. This recognizes that some coxswains begin during the first year of high school, while others do not begin until their fortieth birthday. DO NOT attempt anything discussed in this book unless you have enough experience and skill to handle it. Your attempt at accomplishing something beyond your skill level will backfire when your boat is damaged. When you have questions about the material in this book, ask your coach, rather than guess.

Table of Contents

Chapter 1	**INTRODUCTION**	1
	Interaction with your coach	2
	Personal relationships between a coxswain and an oarsman	4
	Learning how to row yourself	4
	Goals and expected time frame	4
	The first week of practice	5
	The second week of practice	5
	The first month of practice	6
	The first six months of practice	6
	After the first year of coxing	6
Chapter 2	**EQUIPMENT**	7
	The shell	7
	Oars	9
	Oarlocks	9
	Barges	10
	Tanks	10
	Ergometers	10
	Strokewatches	11
	Plastic megaphones	11
	Combined systems	11
	Other combined systems	12
	Heart rate monitors	12
	Trailers	12
Chapter 3	**SAFETY AND PERSONAL EQUIPMENT**	14
	Safety basics	14
	Gear and tools to bring	15
	Other equipment to bring	15
	Rowing and coxing in cold weather	16
	Rowing and coxing in hot weather	16
	Rowing and coxing in wet weather	17
	Handling rough water	17
	What to do if your boat swamps or is involved in an accident	18
Chapter 4	**TERMS**	20
Chapter 5	**COMMANDS**	33

Chapter 6	**COMMUNICATION BASICS AND LAUNCHING**	35
	Who you are and who you are not	35
	How to talk	35
	When to talk	36
	What to say	37
	Interaction with your coach	37
	Interaction with your strokeman	37
	Interaction with the other coxswains	38
	Feedback from others	39
	Launching commands	39
Chapter 7	**STYLE FUNDAMENTALS**	42
	Body positions	43
	From the finish position	43
	Body preparation for the drive	44
	The drive	45
	The blade	46
	Strokerate and slide ratio	47
Chapter 8	**STEERING**	48
	Coxswain visibility and position	48
	Steering fundamentals	49
	When to steer	49
	Where to steer	50
	Wind and currents	50
	Is the rudder really straight?	51
	Maintaining a straight course	51
	Differences in current	52
	Executing a large turn	52
	Spinning your boat (Making a U-turn)	52
	Running over an obstruction	53
Chapter 9	**DRILLS**	54
Chapter 10	**PRACTICING**	58
	Getting ready	58
	The warmup	59
	General comments about practice	59
	Practice as it relates to racing	60
	Boat set	61
	Blade timing	62
	Blade rollup	63
	Blade height	64
	Blade depth	65
	Sloppy catches	65
	Body and hand positions	66

		Slide control	67
		Puddle spacing	68
Chapter 11	**LANDING**		69
		Standard landings with no wind or current	70
		Landings with current/wind	72
		Especially difficult landings	72
		More experienced landings	72
		Removing the boat from the water	74
		Storing your boat	75
Chapter 12	**ON LAND WORKOUTS**		76
		Running	76
		Stadiums	76
		Ergometer training	77
		Ergometer testing	77
		Weights	78
		Tanks	78
Chapter 13	**BEFORE A RACE**		79
		The days before the race	79
		Who coxes what boat?	79
		Packing up for a race	80
		Showing up ready to race	80
		Arriving at the race	81
		The night before	82
		Race morning and breakfast	82
		Pre-race meetings	83
		The weigh-in	83
		How to lose weight	84
		The race officials and the starting time	84
		Preparing to launch	84
		On the water	85
		If involved in an accident	85
Chapter 14	**SPRINT RACING**		86
		Sprint racing basics	86
		Sprint racing strategies	87
		Racing against a vastly superior boat	88
		Racing against a vastly inferior boat	88
		Near the starting line	88
		Lining up at a stationary stakedock start	89
		Two examples of what can go wrong	91
		Lining up at a stationary stakeboat start	91
		Lining up at a floating start	91
		Calling a race	92

	General comments about race steering	93
	Buoyed race steering	94
	Non-buoyed race steering	94
	The start	95
	The settle	96
	The body	96
	The finish	97
Chapter 15	**HEAD RACING**	**98**
	Head racing basics	98
	Head race strategies	99
	Calling a head race	99
	Head race steering	100
	Passing boats/ Being passed	100
Chapter 16	**AFTER A RACE**	**102**
	Post race etiquette	102
	Packing up for the trip home	103
	After a loss	103
	After a victory	103
Chapter 17	**SEAT RACING**	**104**
	Seat racing basics	104
	The coach's role	105
	A sample seat race day	106
	The coxswain's role	108
	Switching oarsmen between boats	108
Chapter 18	**BASIC RIGGING**	**110**
	Rigging fundamentals	110
	Blade pitch	112
	Blade height/depth	112
	Blade load	113
	Foot stretcher settings	113
Chapter 19	**CONCLUSION**	**114**
	Tough times	114
	The years ahead	114

Chapter One

Introduction

A coxswain, what's a coxswain? This inevitable question will be the most common response when you tell your friends and family that you have become one. If you tell them that you have decided to become a horse jockey, at least they may have heard of it. The answer to this inevitable question is challenging to understand for anyone who is unfamiliar with rowing. For many spectators, a coxswain is the little person in the back of the boat who yells *stroke* a lot and is thrown into the water after winning a race. The reality is that this image is only partially correct since it barely scratches the surface of your role as a coxswain. The coxswain's position requires a great deal of knowledge about rowing and is sometimes compared to an assistant coaching position. Certain skills are clearly not needed to become a coxswain:
- One's physical attributes
- Passing any type of physical or mental test
- Prior experience in a related sport - there aren't any.

The skills that are necessary to become a successful coxswain are varied. Coxing involves more than yelling and steering. The skills listed below are difficult to measure directly, but your mastery of them is paramount to your success:
- Teamwork combined with a degree of independence
- Intelligence and self-confidence
- Leadership and perseverance
- An ability to follow directions
- An ability to teach someone twice your size how to row better
- A basic knowledge of seamanship such as the effects of wind and currents upon your course

Figure 1.1. The start of the race.

Chapter One

Figure 1.2 An eight ready to be raced...

It can be debated whether great coxswains are born with the necessary skills or develop them over time. Anyone who does possess the above skills before joining a team will improve at a faster rate. With hard work and dedication, your development will proceed more quickly than other novice coxswains.

> I became involved in coxing as a high school freshman after some very large seniors asked me to join the crew team. I figure if they thought I could be like them, why not. Only when I showed up at the boathouse later that day did I learn that I wasn't there to bulk up.

Most coxswains are introduced to the sport by being in the right place at the right time. Most are chosen strictly for their size as you probably were. From your first day on the water you may be "in charge" of over $20,000 worth of equipment and eight oarsmen. Few coaches find a line of willing candidates outside the boathouse for this position. This is not the football squad.

Novice oarsmen and coxswains are confused by the new terminology, the wide variety of drills and commands, and the effort it takes to row a perfect stroke. As a coxswain, not only do you need to learn all of this, but you must also know it well enough to spread this knowledge to oarsmen. Remember that you are more of a teacher than a drill sergeant.

Though rowing is not the military, it may seem like that to a new coxswain who suddenly finds himself with a lot of "power." If you think this way, you won't last long. You have a lot of responsibility, not "power." Remind yourself of this occasionally throughout your coxing career. It will make your life among the oarsmen a lot more enjoyable, and more important, you will gain their respect.

INTERACTION WITH YOUR COACH

A large part of a coxswain's job involves interaction with his coach(es). Coaches like anyone else have their personal strengths and weaknesses. Some may be very understanding; while others too demanding. Your relationship with the coach will often influence the team's attitude toward you. If your coach treats you like an idiot - whether you really are or not, your team will probably treat you this way. If, on the other hand, your

Introduction

Figure 1.3 ...and your place in it.

coach spends time with you to explain things and relies upon you as an assistant of sorts, your job will be much easier and more enjoyable. Coaches who view their coxswains merely as a sound system usually, and deservedly, face a high turnover of coxswains. The failure to maintain an experienced core of coxswains leads to fewer successes on race day. A high turnover rate also reinforces the same coach's notion that coxswains are worthless since they are always leaving his program.

Just as coxswains often fall into the job, so do some coaches. Rowing used to be a professional sport in the early 1900's with heavy betting on races. Oarsmen and coaches made substantial sums of money for winning. In today's world, no one dreams of becoming rich by being involved in rowing. Very few programs in the United States have paid full time coaches. Coaches often attempt to emulate the coach they once had, when and if they rowed. If his previous coach disliked coxswains, he may often feel the same way about you. You may be treated more as a liability than as the valuable asset you can be. If you could choose your coach, here are some important attributes to look for:

- His or her attempt to introduce you to your job vs. just throwing you in the boat and telling you to ask questions of everyone else for what to do
- The ease of asking your coach a question
- Your coach's experience with rowing
- The team's past success
- The sense of teamwork within the program
- School financial support
- The continuation of experienced coxswains - a coach who seems to have new coxswains every year probably scares them off.

You should always listen to your coach, speak clearly to him so that he understands you, and always ask for clarification if you don't understand what he expects of you. Don't guess or assume anything as a novice.

Chapter One

PERSONAL RELATIONSHIPS BETWEEN A COXSWAIN AND AN OARSMAN

Coaches prefer to have the same sex coxswain as the rowers. In some leagues, this is required. This desire to match the sexes is due to such reasons as: ease of planning trips, locker room problems, and avoiding personal relationships that can bring up questions of favoritism in the boat. Always keep relationships with oarsmen on your same team limited to rowing. A personal relationship cannot stay hidden or separate from the rest of the crew. Even if you can keep the relationship from interfering with your judgement, there is no need for your teammates and coaches to think that you show favoritism toward your boyfriend/girlfriend. No matter how much you deny it, there will always be the impression that you do.

If there is such a greater opportunity for personal/sexual conflict in mixed boats, then why are there mixed boats on the water, in particular female coxswains for men's boats? Weight and size is the answer since women are smaller and lighter on average. In close races with no minimum weight for coxswains, lighter coxswains are a significant advantage and women are, on the average, lighter than men. However, most leagues have minimum weights for coxswains.

LEARNING HOW TO ROW YOURSELF

> I never learned to row in high school and it definitely limited my abilities. I eventually learned in college and eventually row quite well with another coxswain. I also entered a race with a bunch of my fellow college coxswains in a lightweight four head race. While we weren't a threat to anyone, we did learn even more about being a coxswain by competing in a real race.

You cannot become a good coxswain if you have no idea what rowing involves. A good start is to watch videos of experienced crews at the World Championships or Olympics. But learning how to row is the only way to see what it's "really" like for oarsmen. You may not have the chance to row unless you ask for it explicitly. Do not expect to spend a day or two at practice just rowing. Undoubtedly you will be needed to cox, so you may wind up doing double sessions in order to row. Take advantage of every opportunity to learn how to row! Your goal is not to become an expert oarsman, just to understand the fundamentals of the sport particularly early on when no one will expect you to row well.

If you are able to row one day, you will suffer some ribbing from your teammates who will be more than happy to return the same grief that you dish out to them on a daily basis. Now you will understand what it's like to be constantly critiqued. Hopefully, you can row in a coxed boat and listen to what the coxswain is saying. If the coxswain is inexperienced, figure out what demonstrates his inexperience and think what you would do in his place. If the coxswain is experienced, figure out what demonstrates his experience and observe how he runs his boat. If you can only row by switching places with an oarsman for the last mile of practice, ignore the abuse and instead, attempt to master the motions of rowing.

GOALS AND EXPECTED TIME FRAME

> It took me 3 years to be truly comfortable on the water practicing and racing.

Your goal, literally, is to get wet. The tradition of throwing the winning coxswain into the water after a race is something to look forward to except in high pollution or arctic areas, of course. You will probably train for some time before you begin the racing season. As in any sport, you will need to learn the basics. After a few months of mastering the terminology and motions of a stroke, you should be able to spot and correct problems. In case you like to set your goals high, most Olympic coxswains have more than eight years of experience. Be prepared for years of racing before you reach the top. Most learning by varsity coxswains comes from experience on the water, not explanations from a book (yes, even this one). Since it is very rare

Introduction

to race more than fifteen times a year, it can take several seasons to gain the racing experience necessary to be a great coxswain.

THE FIRST WEEK OF PRACTICE

Your coach may spend the first few days or weeks of the season at the gym or boathouse teaching novices the basics of rowing on an erg. Though you will learn very little about what a coxswain does by sitting inside a gym or on a dock, you can still learn something. By paying attention to your coach, you will learn the basic motions, drills, and commands of rowing much more quickly than you would by being thrown into a boat as a novice coxswain. Do not be surprised if you are totally confused during the first few weeks of practice. Utilize any opportunity you have to row on the **ergometers** or in the **tanks**. Your coach may also ask you to spot problems that novice oarsmen may be having. He may do this to test your knowledge of technique, your ability to spot errors, and your speed in implementing the necessary corrections, so do not use this time indoors to doze off into space, or to talk to your fellow teammates about the big history quiz.

If your program is fortunate enough to have a training **barge**, oarsmen will not have to worry about the unstableness of the shell. They can then concentrate on the motions of their stroke. Your coach will not be able to teach you how to steer or land on a barge. Your time on a barge is similar to your time indoors in tanks - you learn what the basic commands are while you watch novices learn to row. Though the barge will not travel very far, also learn as much as you can about the traffic pattern and obstructions on the lake or river.

During the first week of practice on the water (not the first five or six days spent in the launch, but actually in the stern of a shell), learn the following:

- How to get the shell out of the boathouse and into the water (see Chapter Six, Communication Basics and Launching)
- The basic commands of rowing - **Weigh enough**, **Let it run**, **Ready (all)... row**, **On this one** (see Chapter Five, Commands)
- The boat groupings - Bow pair/four/six, Middle pair/four/six, Stern pair/four/six, All four/eight
- Basic terms about the boat - **Port**, **Starboard**, **Bow**, **Stern**, **Blade**, **Slide**, **Seat**, **Rigger**, **Fin**, **Rudder** (see Chapter Four, Terms)
- How to steer the boat with the **rudder**, i.e. "which way do I push the **toggles** to go to starboard?" (see Chapter Eight, Steering)
- The basic traffic pattern of the water you row on - Stay to the left/ right, row on the near/far side of the lake, etc...
- A few basic drills - **the pick drill**, **X and glide drill**, **1-2-3 drill** (see Chapter Nine, Drills)

In larger programs with a large number of novices, the coach may mix novice and experienced rowers together for several weeks to protect his boat. The thought of eight novice oarsmen and a novice coxswain in a shell can send chills down a coach's spine. You might head the wrong way up a river into oncoming traffic or over a rock that no one in the boat knows about. If you cox a boat full of experienced oarsmen who have no need for what you say, do not sit there and attempt to "survive" the day. Use this time to ask the experienced strokeman lots of questions and give some basic commands even though it may seem strange to you.

THE SECOND WEEK OF PRACTICE

After learning the basics during the first week, your time during the second week on the water should be spent attempting to master the following:

- The names of the athletes. Calling someone by his number becomes highly annoying. Hopefully, most oarsmen will know your name also, rather than calling you "cox" or "coxie"
- The fundamentals of a basic workout such as the typical drills the coach uses in order to train novice oarsmen

Chapter One

- The danger areas of the water that exist such as shallow areas, buoys, submerged rocks and logs
- The fundamental motions of rowing (see Chapter Seven, Fundamentals)

Memorize the basic landing pattern so that you will be able to hold your own if your coach is not there one day. Try to talk to the other coxswains in the program when you are not at the boathouse being distracted by everything going on around you. Ask them their ideas on how to steer on the water you row and any quirks of the course, the coach, and/or the team. Hopefully, after two weeks, you will have realized the difficulty involved in mastering the stroke, in addition to coxing. Your visions of making the National team the following year should have been dashed by now.

THE FIRST MONTH OF PRACTICE

By the end of the first month on the water, a novice coxswain should be able to run a practice by himself. No sudden bursts of improvement should be expected from these practices; just the ability to come up with a variety of drills to handle whatever is needed that day. Be familiar with most of the rowing terms, commands, and drills listed in this book. Test your knowledge by writing them down. Know the shallow areas and obstructions on the course you cox. You should own a toolbag with most of the required supplies listed in Chapter Three, Safety and Personal Equipment. A novice coxswain should at this point be able to describe the basic style of rowing in some detail.

Hopefully by now, your coach has already talked to you several times to explain style, courses, practice plans, etc... If he has not done so for a while, seek him out to ask questions that you may have. If you do not ask many questions, he might feel you already know the answers. Coaches do not mind answering a coxswain's questions as long they have not already done so. A coxswain's question needs one clear answer once, not several answers because you forgot the original one.

THE FIRST SIX MONTHS OF PRACTICE

After six months, a coxswain should have been effective in several races. This does not imply that effective coxing always results in a win. Good boats are beaten by better teams, and sometimes by worse teams. Effective coxing means fewer mistakes, fewer repetitions of explanations because you are clear the first time about what you want, and a beginning sense of what the coach wants even before he expresses it.

A routine should have been established that allows you to run through a workout without spending too much time thinking about what drills are appropriate. The beginning of an innate feeling as to what is wrong with a boat will assist your actions and decisions in the boat. Your coach may also begin to seek out your views on what is wrong with a boat and what you recommend to improve the situation. After six months you should sense that the novice oarsmen are willing to ask for your opinions on their style because you do have something intelligent and helpful to say.

AFTER THE FIRST YEAR OF COXING

At the end of the first year, you should have enough experience to point out errors that both novice and experienced oarsmen make. Experienced oarsmen should also trust you enough to listen and respond to your comments although they may disagree. A full year of coxing will also familiarize you with the routine of rowing - longer races in the fall, land training during the winter, shorter races in the spring and summer. All of the drills and commands should be familiar to you. You may begin to learn the basics of rigging as well.

Coxswains do not develop at the same rate. Someone who is very interested in the sport and has the intelligence and drive to succeed will become an "experienced" coxswain within two or three years. Someone who does not have these qualities may never achieve this "status." The choice is up to you.

Chapter Two

Equipment

Your ability to win races will partly depend upon the quality of your equipment. A team with equipment that is old and frequently breaks will be at a major disadvantage on race day when a key part breaks. Spare parts are very expensive and coaches do not appreciate coxswains who find new rocks or drag fins across the dock. The total value of equipment that a coxswain is in charge of at one time may be over $20,000. In addition to keeping an eye on the condition of their equipment, coxswains are responsible for washing the gear. Equipment used in salt water should be rinsed with fresh water daily to prevent corrosion. Equipment used in fresh water should be rinsed several times a month to remove any pollution.

THE SHELL

The equipment to be concerned about most is the shell. You should wash it when necessary, keep an eye on the hull to spot problems before they appear - such as a slowly growing crack in a rigger, and notify the coach when a problem arises so that it can be fixed before something breaks. There are several brands of racing shells, but fewer today than in the past. Common racing shell manufacturers are Alden, Aylings, Empacher, Kaschper, Kings, Pocock, Schoenbrod, Stampfli, Resolute, Vespoli, and old Carbocrafts - a forerunner of Vespoli. Each shell design is different and must be cared for accordingly.

The most common type of shell that you will cox will be an eight oarsmen / one coxswain boat called an **eight** and a four oarsmen / one coxswain boat called a **four with** or just a **four**. These boats are **sweep** boats since each oarsman has only one oar (also called a sweep). **Sculling** boats are those in which each oarsman has two oars (also called sculls) that are smaller than sweep blades. (see **Figure 2.3**) Sculling boats do not have coxswains except for an occasional training boat. The following is a list of the types of shells and their corresponding names:

Oarsmen	Sweep w/o cox	Sweep w/cox	Scull all no cox (-)
1	N/A	N/A	1X , Single
2	2- , Pair w/o	2+ , Pair with	2X , Double
4	4- , Four w/o	4+ , Four with	4X , Quad(ruple)
8	N/A	8+ , Eight	N/A

N/A = not available, + = with, - or w/o = without

As mentioned before, there are other versions of boats, but you will rarely see them raced or even on the water. To help train more scullers, 4X+ and 8X+ do exist and are called a coxed quad or quad with and an **octuple**. Many eights are manufactured as **sectionals** so that they can be taken apart in 2 pieces for travel to races. Teams that only use vans, rather than trailers, to transport their eights must use sectional eights. To create a waterproof seal between the sections, petroleum jelly is applied on each end of the sections before the sections are bolted together.

For experienced teams that do not need much guidance from a coxswain, a bow-coxed shell allows the coxswain to see and steer the course much better. The coxswain is in a "lie down" position and steers the boat

Chapter Two

Figure 2.1 This bow has been patched a few times.

Figure 2.2 The coxswain's seat in a box-coxed boat. The rudder is controlled by the bar in the middle.

using a bar in front of his chest connected by long cables to the rudder bar in the stern. (see **Figure 2.2**) Tall coxswains may not fit in some bow-coxed boats, while shorter coxswains may find themselves sliding up and down the coxswain compartment. Shorter coxswains should put blocks of styrafoam in the compartment so that their feet will be resting against something.

The constant technological innovations of racing shells have created a competition to produce the lightest and most hydrodynamic shape on the water. Once one team has equipment that is supposedly faster, other teams rush to buy it. In the first stage of shell development, all boats were made out of wood with "beaver tail fins". (see **Figure 8.1**) They survive today as waterlogged 300+ pounds of wood that can take more than eight people to lift them. These hulls are highly susceptible to rot and decay. Inevitably, novices use these boats. The next stage in shell development focused on the use of fiberglass which eliminated weight and had the advantage of being more resistant to water, particularly salt water, and easier to repair if a coxswain decided to explore the uncharted areas of a river and found new rocks. Fiberglass boats are still manufactured.

The most recent stage of shell development has focused upon carbon fiber and honeycomb technology. These materials increase durability and rigidity in addition to creating the lightest shells around. Durability is an important concern for obvious reasons. Rigidity is just as important though. Two shells of similar shape and weight will be unequal competitors if one shell is more flexible. A flexible shell wastes energy applied to the oars by flexing before the hull moves forward. The drawback to rigidity is that a rigid hull is less forgiving to a coxswain who hits something.

To reduce the technology war, weight minimums have been imposed in most categories of boats. Sectional boats are now required in many leagues. These restrictions have reduced the endless push toward even lighter and more expensive shells. Recent designs have included extremely hydrodynamic hull shapes that reduce water resistance. The dynamics of a shell are different from motorboats in that the power used to propel a shell is not applied continuously from an engine, but rhythmically from oars moving in and out of the water. The bow of a typical boat lifts out of the water during the drive and settles back in during the recovery. More experienced boats can keep their bows from sinking back into the water too far at the finish. This demonstrates that a boat has extremely clean finishes with few or no oarsmen out of time at the finish. Novice boats may show a more pronounced settling into the water at each finish, and may not even show any surge forward.

Equipment

OARS

In the early 1980's fiberglass oars began to replace the older, wooden oars that simultaneously reduced their weight and increased the durability. Some newer oars also include carbon fiber in their construction to further reduce the weight and increase the stiffness. These types of oars are called **ultralights**. The latest development in oar technology is the development of modified spoon shapes such as an asymmetrical shape called **hatchet** blades. (see **Figure 2.3**) Such modified designs allow more efficient use of power along with smoother finishes and catches.

Figure 2.3 Three blade types - Hatchet sweep, regular sweep, and regular scull.

> I once snapped an oar in half by hitting a stakeboat on a river when I wasn't paying attention to what was in front of me. In a split second, it became an expensive rowing souvenir. Another time a team I rowed for lost a set of oars after they were run over by a baggage truck at the airport. The airline did ask if we could tape them back together and still use them.

Fortunately for coxswains, oars need very little maintenance. An occasional glance by coxswains will spot any problems. Oars are relatively impervious to damage. An oar may break occasionally due to a factory defect, but coxswains are more likely to break them by hitting something. Damage generally results in little likelihood of repair. The only adjustable parts on most oars are the **collar** and a removable wear plate. The collar should always be tight. The coach handles care and adjustment of the collars since this affects rigging.

Most oars used in the United States are made in Morrisville, VT by **Dreissigacker Racing Oars**, a division of **Concept II**, the ergometer manufacturers. Their testing of the newer blade designs has produced an answer to the question "Do these new designs really make me go faster?" The answer depends upon who you are - lightweight or heavyweight, male or female, rowing conditions, as well as individual preference. Since coxswains do not buy oars, worry about getting the blades to mimic each other, not what blade design you feel your boat should be using.

OARLOCKS

Oarlocks are almost as important as the oars for a successful row. A loose fitting oarlock will cause the oar to wiggle in place and be hard to control. A tight oarlock will constrict the roll of the blade. Most oarlocks have a nut on the **gate** which will tighten or loosen the oarlock. Apply a thin coating of petroleum jelly to all oarlocks every month or so for lubrication.

Dreissigacker has introduced new oarlocks that are usable on older riggers. They are more likely to hold the oar in the two correct positions of the blade - horizontal and vertical. With this design, there is a more noticeable and cleaner "thunk" at the finish as the oars rotate into the proper horizontal position. Coxswains should listen to this noise to detect not only finish timing, but also the quickness of the feather. The most unique feature of these oarlocks is the removable plastic inserts on the top and bottom of the oarlock which change the **pitch**. Once the **pin** is set, it never needs to be adjusted. Different degrees of pitch are built in the plastic inserts. To adjust the pitch of the oarlock, a coach only has to change the inserts.

Chapter Two

Figure 2.4 A training barge made by bolting two old, wooden eights together.

BARGES

Larger teams will often use a barge for several weeks at the beginning of the season to train novices. Barges are designed to provide a slow, stable platform on which oarsmen can learn to row without worrying about the set. Most barges are designed with a center walkway on which a coach can walk to explain the rowing style and correct problems. Barges are not designed to provide steering training for coxswains. While on a barge, coxswains should pay attention to the proper course they will steer in the future. Coxswains should also use this time to learn the basic commands and rowing style that the coach prefers. You may feel bored on a barge since your coach will be doing most of the talking, but this is a good time to learn the rowing style without much pressure. If there is an extra seat in the barge and you are not needed to steer, jump in it and learn to row.

TANKS

A few rowing programs have indoor rowing tanks that attempt to duplicate rowing on water. Tanks allow coaches to train novices and experienced oarsmen just like on a barge, but without having to worry about the weather. The more advanced tanks have a pumping system to circulate the water to approximate water flowing by the boat. Most tanks are just that, tanks of still water. Oars used in stationary tanks are smaller than normal blades. To reduce the load on the blade, a hole is cut in the center of oars or the end of the blade is cut off. While most tanks do not give an exact simulation of being on the water, it is close enough to be able to learn a great deal. On stationary water tanks, it will be more challenging to keep the finish of the stroke clean and quick.

ERGOMETERS

Ergometers are machines that attempt to simulate the motions of rowing. There are two basic designs of ergometers - total simulation and drive simulation. The total simulation design simulates all of the motions of the stroke by using a shortened oar attached to the equipment. This design is more complicated and expensive, but permits coxswains and coaches to observe all of the motions of an oarsman. The drive simulation design is less complicated, cheaper, and is the most common. It is used to focus on power application. This design does not require an oarsman to roll his hands or lean sideways into the rigger at the catch and the finish, but does require proper hand levels and bow to stern body motions.

The most popular ergometer in the United States is made by Concept II in Morrisville, VT. Concept II also manufactures the popular Dreissigacker oars. Occasional maintenance on these models is limited to lubrication of the moving parts, a cleaning of the silver rail, cleaning any dirt off the magnetic sensor near the wheel, replacement of dead batteries, and tightening of loose parts. Do not allow any oarsman to let go of the oar handle at the finish since it may whip into the flywheel and break the machine.

Equipment

STROKEWATCHES

Strokewatches measure the **strokerate**, the number strokes per minute. The precision is usually to 1/2 stroke (per minute). Strokewatches use from a one to a five-stroke base to calibrate properly. The greater number of strokes that a strokewatch uses to calculate a reading, the more accurate that strokewatch is. When using a three-stroke base strokewatch, a coxswain or coach starts the strokewatch when a certain point is reached in the stroke - typically the catch since it's the easiest to see, and waits for three catches before stopping it. On strokewatches of other stroke calibrations, a different number of strokes is counted.

Some strokewatches require the stroke button to be depressed every stroke, but to account for any mistakes, continuously average out the last three, four, or five readings. The use of different stroke calibrations and averaging occurs because fingers and the person they are attached to are not always accurate. If you use a one-stroke calibration strokewatch with no averaging, you might not push the stop/start button at the correct moment. This inaccuracy could result in a faulty reading off by several strokes per minute. A strokerate of 34 is a lot different than a 36. Averaging the individual strokerates allows an immediate display, while still taking into account the variances of humans who are not always accurate. Yes, that includes coxswains, too. When using a strokewatch, hang it around your neck for safekeeping. If you use it in cold weather, use gloves rather than mittens so you can easily push the buttons.

PLASTIC MEGAPHONES

All coxswains should have at least a plastic megaphone if they do not have an electronic amplification system. A sound amplifier is the most useful piece of equipment a coxswain can have. A megaphone will prevent you from constantly having a hoarse, scratchy voice and will allow everyone in the boat to hear from you, particularly in an eight. If there is nothing to amplify your voice, louder coxswains will drown out your words during races. You will also become a big fan of ice cream to soothe your constant sore throat. Most megaphones have straps that hold it on your head against your lips. Some coxswains prefer to hold the megaphone in their hands, rather than deal with the straps. This choice is up to you since it does not affect sound quality, though there is always the chance that you might drop it. Holding a megaphone can also tie up your hands when you need to steer or do other things. If your megaphone has a metal mouthpiece, wrap white tape around it so that your lips will not stick to it in cold weather.

COMBINED SYSTEMS

• **Chronostroke™, Cox-Box™, and PaceCoach® are trademarks of the Nielsen-Kellerman Company.** •

Most teams purchase a combination electronic sound amplification and strokewatch. Turn up the volume switch only until each oarsman can hear you clearly. On cold days, wrap a sweatshirt around the base unit so the batteries will last longer. Do not carry a sound system by the microphone. These systems determine the strokerate automatically with a sensor placed under the seat of the strokeman and a magnet attached to his seat. The primary manufacturer of combined systems is Nielsen-Kellerman.

<u>To contact Nielsen-Kellerman Company:</u>
Nielsen-Kellerman Company
104 West 15th Street
Chester, PA 19013 USA
(610) 447-1555

In the late 1970's Nielsen-Kellerman began to manufacture sound systems for rowing. These systems consisted of an enclosed battery in a buoyant can, a waterproof microphone on a headband, and several waterproof speakers. The first models were called SA80 which only amplified sound, and Cox-Box™ 80 for the year of introduction, 1980. Nielsen-Kellerman's basic speaker and wiring design has not changed much, though their equipment has become smaller, more advanced, and more reliable. In 1984, a smaller can for the batteries was introduced and the display was modified to include a stroke counter. In 1990, a memory system was incorporated into the same size can to allow teams to recall at a later time the strokerates for the first 10 minutes of a piece.

In 1992 Nielsen-Kellerman introduced a speed sensor to measure the speed of the boat through the water and incorporated it into a new display and sound system called the PaceCoach®. This display is compatible with the older Cox-Box™ wiring harnesses. The PaceCoach® is a plastic box which contains the computer chips, batteries, and amplifier. Wired to this display is a removable sensor fin which is dragged through the water to measure speed and distance rowed. The sensor fin can be permanently attached through the hull or clamped onto the gunwale to allow switching between boats. Though the sensor fin cannot be clogged by floating debris, leaves or sticks that wrap around it should be removed. The PaceCoach® also has a memory feature that stores workout data for review after practice.

OTHER COMBINED SYSTEMS

In 1992 B+G Rowing, Ltd. introduced a now discontinued stroke and speed measuring system, the SpeedBoss that was partially compatible with Nielsen-Kellerman products. The SpeedBoss measured boat speed with a miniature propeller on the hull. The display unit has an adjustable dial for the coxswain to change the information displayed.

There is equipment now being developed that will be able to display the force applied by each oarsman on the footboards. This equipment will present a graph for the coxswain to display the time when the catch was initiated, who is early or late, total force applied, and a power curve graph to show if any oarsman faded on the drive. Coaches will then have information on who applies the most power on the water before starting seat racing. This equipment will most likely reduce the need for seat racing, but definitely not eliminate it. Coaches will still not have a scientific display of who applies force effectively, only who does it on time. Will this equipment produce an information overload for you or the coach? Who knows, just read the manuals.

HEART RATE MONITORS

A simple way of measuring physical performance for advanced crews is to use heart rates. A higher than expected heart rate can indicate that an athlete is either rowing too hard for that piece or is out of shape. Direct comparisons of individual heart rates are useless, because each person has a different natural heart rate. To measure heart rates, count to six while the oarsmen count their own heart rates and then multiply the result by ten. Do not count the first heartbeat.

For more accurate measurement of heart rates, heart monitors are available. These devices which are strapped on the chest measure the electrical signals given off by the heart and transmit this information to a separate display watch. Coxswains typically do not have access to this information because the radio waves are often not strong enough to reach a display watch placed near the coxswain. The coxswain must instead ask each oarsman with a monitor to tell him his heart rate to keep track of the workout. If you have the same person in your boat on most days, use his heart rate as a baseline to determine the stress of the workouts.

TRAILERS

Trailers transport equipment to races. Trailer designs range from converted trucks with racks on top to units specifically designed for this purpose. (see **Figure 2.5**) Programs that only row in fours or have sectional eights may only use vans with strong roof racks. Anytime you load a boat, the ribs of the boat should rest as closely as possible to the rack bars. The trailer should be loaded from top to bottom, center to outside. If you use sectional boats, the pointed ends should face forward, not the flat ends. Wipe off any petroleum jelly on the sectional ends before you depart so they do not become covered with dirt. Tie a few red flags (red rags are fine) onto any parts that extend beyond either end of your van or trailer. Your coach will handle most of the details of loading the trailer, but you should help him out as much as possible.

Equipment

A primary responsibility of coxswains, at least in coaches' eyes, is the care of the equipment in the boathouse. Since you are personally responsible for everything that happens to your shell, whether it be your fault or not, immediately attend to any problem in the boat. Never neglect routine care such as an occasional washing of the boat and blades (daily if you row in salty or brackish water), recharging of the electronic equipment, and the airing out of each compartment. Do not neglect less routine maintenance such as washing the **tracks** with a lubricant, an application of a lubricant to rubber plugs on the electronic equipment (to prolong their flexibility), and a once over with your eyes to spot any cracks or splits developing on the boat, riggers, or oars. The proper time to spot problems with a boat is before something breaks.

Figure 2.5 A trailer capable of holding 9 eights.

Chapter Three

Safety and Personal Equipment

• This chapter includes only a brief safety summary. It is highly recommended that every coxswain and oarsman watch a safety video before learning the sport. •

Rowing is an extremely safe sport. The rare physical injuries are usually due to training errors, lack of a sufficient warm-up, or coxswain error. Nevertheless, safety is a paramount concern of the rowing community. Since rowing safety includes bringing the correct equipment with you, personal equipment that a coxswain should have is covered in this chapter.

SAFETY BASICS

The first line of safety for rowers, coxswains, and coaches is to learn how to swim. Most people learn how to swim by the age of five or six, but there are still some who do not know how. Each rowing program should hold a swim test before going onto the water. Unfortunately, some programs ignore this rule.

The second line of safety is the coach. He should have enough life preservers on his launch to assist a boat in trouble. His attitude to the sport should involve a sense of caution when facing unknown or potentially dangerous weather conditions. A gung-ho coach who cares little that your boat is taking on water is someone you may not want to risk your life with.

The third line of safety is common sense on your part. When your coach is late due to bad weather delaying traffic on the highways, why launch your boat in the same weather? If the weather is so bad that cars are delayed, do not row in a fragile boat and expect a safe row without a launch following you. Being hit by debris flying down an overflowing river should not elicit a response of "Well, we will pay more attention next time." There should not be a next time. The correct response is "Wow, that was really dumb. We should not have been out there." Rowing in stormy weather when lightning is around is asking for trouble, just as is rowing on a river flooded by yesterday's heavy rains.

When on the water, always row in sight of the shoreline so that you have something to orient yourself with. Row with a launch following you or another shell nearby. Each launch should carry enough life jackets for each person. If a launch is unavailable to follow you, be extra careful. The fact that nothing happened the day before when you took the team on an excursion tour of the lake does not rule out the chance that something could happen today.

> I have been swamped several times either due to waves, or rough water. Once I ran over something below the surface of the water and the fin was shoved through the hull. The coach took out the stern pair oarsmen and left myself to cox the remaining six oarsmen home. The water was above my waist due to the flooding. The boat took several days to repair.

Few coxswains encounter a serious accident during their rowing experiences. Their boat may flood due to an obnoxious powerboat, the fin may be shoved through the hull upon discovering a new rock, or a rigger

Safety and Personal Equipment

may break unexpectedly. Catastrophes such as boats hitting bridges, boats hitting other boats, or boats being hit by other powerboats are very rare. In one incident, a sculler was killed by a motorboat whose driver could not see him in the sun's glare on the river's surface. Almost all accidents are preventable. Paying attention to the river traffic, following the prescribed course, and maintaining a general sense of caution goes a long way in avoiding dangerous incidents. Hopefully you will never be involved in an accident. If you do find yourself involved in an accident, knowing what to do can prevent anything more from occurring than wet oarsmen or minor damage to the boat.

GEAR AND TOOLS TO BRING
• **No one expects you to have all of the following tools and gear on your first day.** •

Whenever teams travel on trips, it is easy to spot the coxswain's bags - they're about twice the size and weight of everyone else's. Coxswains are responsible for carrying with them a basic set of tools and supplies for minor adjustments and emergency repairs. Most of your initial equipment will be leftovers and handouts from the coach. Within a few weeks though, begin slowly gathering what you need by buying it at a hardware store if your coach does not have any spares. Or obtain extras from other coxswains, but do not steal tools and supplies from them as you will inevitably suffer as they refuse to help the local thief.

Every coxswain should have a small toolbag to carry necessary gear around with them. Store this toolbag in the same place every day so that oarsmen who need tape and such can find it easily. It should also be rather worthless so you will not have to be concerned about its appearance. A backpack is too large and will get in the way; a waist pack is too small to hold water bottles.

Basic equipment to have in your toolbag during workouts and races includes:
- Two or three quart/liter size water bottles if everyone is not responsible for their own water
- Two or three wrenches of the most commonly used sizes, usually 7/16", 1/2", and 3/4" or 10mm and 11mm
- An adjustable wrench to handle the odd-sized nuts
- Several rolls of white athletic tape and a roll or two of black electrical tape to repair minor problems and to adjust **pitch** on the blade
- A **douger** and a few **shims**
- Sunscreen for very sunny days / Trash bags for storage of clothes on wet days

Shims are small plastic squares that raise or lower the **height** of the **rigger**. They are placed between the hull and either the upper or lower rigger **mainstays**. To raise the height of the rigger, place a shim(s) on the bottom rigger bolt; to lower the height of the rigger, place a shim(s) on the top rigger bolt. Do not use more than two shims on a rigger as it will change the pitch of the oarlock.

A wingnut loosener, called a **douger**, allows an oarsman to get a better grip on tight wingnuts. Dougers are easy to make. Drill a hole in the center of one end of a 2" diameter stick of wood, and then cut a groove crosswise on the same end. The groove should cross through the hole so that the wings of a wingnut will fit into the groove and the bolt will fit in the center hole.

OTHER EQUIPMENT TO BRING

A basic wristwatch is something every coxswain must own. It must be waterproof and have a second hand to time pieces and to measure heart rates and strokerates. Your watch should be shockproof since a valuable watch will be destroyed. A running watch is best since it has a stopwatch and is usually shockproof and waterproof. Teams that row very early or late in the day often have lights as part of the standard equipment on the boat. You may want to have a flashlight as a backup along with a spare set of batteries. A whistle will also help you to warn off anyone who may not see you and attract attention if your boat is in distress. A reflective vest will increase your visibility to other boats.

Chapter Three

For programs that often face rough water while rowing, a pump is considered basic safety equipment. A stack of **splashguards** is also helpful. Oarsmen who have extra time can install the splashguards before practice rather than waste time searching through the boathouse for some. See Handling Rough Water later in this chapter for a more thorough description of splashguards.

ROWING AND COXING IN COLD WEATHER

Rowing is not a glamour sport and neither are the conditions that practice can occur in. Teams train in conditions that range from below freezing to above 100 degrees. Take precautions not only for safety reasons, but also to maximize the workout. A shivering oarsman is a safety risk for hypothermia and a lousy oarsman. He is more worried about staying warm than what his blade rollup looks like. A shivering coxswain will not be understood by his teammates and may be distracted enough to not notice an obstruction. If you are not rowing all eight, rotate the oarsmen to keep them warm.

Hypothermia is a chilling of the body's core temperature to unacceptably low levels. Even though an oarsman is working out, he may still need to wear a sweater or jacket. When an oarsman is not rowing, he should put on a sweatshirt and/or a windbreaker to keep warm. If an oarsman tells you that he is cold and cannot stop shivering, he is in the first stage of hypothermia. Stop rowing and allow him to put some of his warmup clothes back on. If an oarsman is having trouble hearing you and is so cold that he has stopped shivering, the oarsman is in the next stage of hypothermia. Get him to shore immediately and warm him up with dry clothes and blankets.

To protect against the cold, oarsmen and coxswains should wear layers of clothes. Oarsmen need to be more concerned about the bulk of clothes than coxswains since heavy sweats will interfere with rowing. Coxswains need to wear more layers than oarsmen since they are not staying warm by rowing. Thin layers of polypropylene and Lifa™ are appropriate for oarsmen and coxswains. Coxswains can layer even more with undershirts, turtlenecks, and long underwear. A windbreaker to deflect the wind and spray should be the outermost layer of clothes for oarsmen and coxswains. The best windbreaker material is Gore-Tex™ which resists water, but also breathes. A wool hat and scarf should top it all off since most heat loss occurs from the scalp. Earmuffs may be helpful in very cold weather, but will deaden the sounds of the boat.

Gloves are impractical on the water for oarsmen to protect hands from cold, but bags that cover the oar handle and the hands are useful. They are called **pogies**. Unless you use a strokewatch, wear mittens rather than gloves since rudder cables can usually be gripped just as easily. An additional liner of polypropylene is helpful on very cold days.

You may want to wear glasses to protect your eyes from the sun's glare, water spray, and cold wind. Boots get in the way, so a good pair of sneakers with a pair of wool socks will help. A plastic freezer bag over the sneakers isn't a great fashion statement, but does protect your feet from water and cold air. Zip up the freezer bag as tight as possible. When there are too many sweats to store in front of you or when the extra weight isn't wanted on race day, dump them into a launch. Bring a garbage bag so that they do not get wet. After the workout or race is over, the oarsmen can put their sweats back on to stay warm until you land.

ROWING AND COXING IN HOT WEATHER

Water is key to preventing heat exhaustion in hot weather. Bring at least 50% more water than you think you could possibly need. On very hot days you should bring at least a gallon of water for an eight. Lack of water not only affects performance, but also safety. Everyone should drink lots of water, including yourself. Lengthy warm-ups won't be necessary. Everyone should have a sun hat and sunglasses to reflect the glare and sunscreen to prevent sunburn. A wet hat will keep the body even cooler. When you stop to water down or to listen to directions from your coach, stop in shady areas near shore or under bridges. Every bit of shade helps. Oarsmen can also cool themselves by dragging their feet in the water after you stop. An oarsman who has a

Safety and Personal Equipment

bad sunburn, seems incoherent, or whose skin feels cold and clammy is probably entering the first stages of sunstroke/ heat prostration and should be brought to shore immediately in a launch to cool off.

On a hot race day the weight of the water bottles should not be a concern since the extra water can always be dumped overboard before a race. Do not dump out all of the water at the start since extra water weighs only ounces. At least one bottle should be kept for after the race. Carrying an extra quart of water will not prevent you from winning a race, but might help an oarsman who passes out afterwards.

ROWING AND COXING IN WET WEATHER

Oarsmen do not need to be concerned about getting wet if it's warm. They're probably sweating anyway. However, nothing ruins a coxswain's concentration faster than feeling like a wet sponge. Wearing wet clothes on a cold day will also increase heat loss and cause you to feel like an ice cube. Wool clothes wick water away from the body and retain more body heat than other wet materials such as cotton. A single layer of water-repellant fabric such as Gore-Tex™ or a vinyl covered poncho will stop most of the rain and waves. In driving rain, it's best to have two layers or more of rain stopping outerwear. Water-<u>resistant</u> material will <u>not</u> keep you dry. Water-resistant material is worthless when it seems that someone is standing above you with a hose. Water-<u>repellant</u> is what you need. A regular raincoat usually will not work because water will leak down the zipper seam. A poncho is a better choice to repel rain. If you do not have a poncho, the best "garment" to put over yourself is a trash bag with a hole torn in it for your head. Fashion forward it's not; water stopping it is.

Sunglasses or a hat will prevent rain from blowing into your eyes. Plastic freezer bags on your feet will keep them warm and dry. If there is room in your toolbag, bring big plastic trash bags along with you to store your teammates extra clothes. Running home in wet sweats pleases few oarsmen. The fact that you tried to keep their clothes dry may lead at least some oarsmen to think that you care about their well-being.

HANDLING ROUGH WATER

• <u>**DO NOT**</u> cross any large wave head on! •

You will eventually face rough water; some crews more than others. Rowing in a life jacket would simply not work and there is little room to store up to nine life jackets in a shell. Fortunately, most shells will float even if both bow and stern compartments are flooded though the boat will not support much weight before it begins to sink. In an emergency, oars can be used flotation devices.

Incidents that cause the boat to fill with water, **swampings**, are the most common "accidents" that occur. Swampings can be caused by water skiers taking too close of a look at you, powerboat owners cruising by too fast, large waves, rowing in rough water, a hole in the boat, heavy rain, or another coach who does not realize you are behind him in the wash of his launch. Reduce the number of swampings by paying attention to the water around you. If you row where rough water is common, bring a pump, bailer or sponges in your toolbag.

The proper way to handle a very large wave headed toward you is to stop rowing and turn the boat to cross the waves parallel. Change the set of the boat so that the side which will be hit by the wave first is higher than the other side. If you do cross a very large wave head on, your boat will fill with water and may split in half due to the height of the wave. This does happen. You may not want to stop a workout for a wave, but a wave big enough to be a safety concern will throw off the rhythm of your boat and will ruin that part of the workout anyway.

Splashguards reduce swampings caused by rowing in rough water. They are usually made of plastic and are taped onto the **hull** and the **rigger**. If plastic splashguards are unavailable, use athletic or duct tape to cover some of the space between the mainstay and backstay. Splashguards do not have to cover the entire triangular space between the hull and the riggers to be effective. Only the first few inches of space around a rigger attachment point to the hull need a splashguard. Most boats have a small lip along the gunwale's outer edge

Chapter Three

that helps to deflect smaller waves. Splashguards extend this protection. If you are rowing on rough water without splashguards, your bowman will be sure to let you know as he will complain continuously about being soaked. Attach splashguards before launching since it is easier to do then and will not tie up any practice time.

In rough conditions row at **gunwale** high height to prevent blades from smacking on top of the waves and throwing the set off even further. To stabilize the set, reduce the slide to only 3/4 or 1/2 so there is less time when the blades are out of the water. You may need one side of the boat to lower their hands and the other side to raise them to keep one side of the boat higher than the incoming waves. If all eight rowing at 3/4 or 1/2 slide is difficult, drop out a pair or four and hold the boat stable while the remaining oarsmen row at full or 3/4 slide. Warn the boat when larger waves will hit so that oarsmen can expect the impact and avoid having their fingers smashed between the oar handle and the gunwale. If the conditions continue to worsen, call it a day.

WHAT TO DO IF YOUR BOAT SWAMPS OR IS INVOLVED IN AN ACCIDENT
• **The standard distress signal is to raise one or two oars in the air vertically.** •

If a boat does become swamped enough to be a safety concern, try to row to a calmer area and bail, sponge, or pump out the water or row to the nearest dock or shore to lift the hull and dump out the water inside the hull. Do not lift the boat as it is usually done. The weight of the trapped water may separate the hull from the keel and ribs. Lifting the boat may not even be possible due to the weight of the water. For most swampings, the hull should be lifted and rolled almost immediately at waist height or lower. Roll the hull away from the oarsmen to prevent the team from being soaked. Bunching up the oarsmen at either end of the boat will also keep them dryer.

When a boat is thoroughly swamped and cannot be rowed, wait for assistance from a launch nearby. If no one immediately realizes you need help, hold one or two of the oars vertically in the air to attract attention. If no one still sees you and the oarsmen are already wet, try to move the boat toward the nearest shore by swimming or rowing while still holding onto the boat. If the water or air is cold and no one is totally drenched yet, waiting for help in the boat is a better idea than risking hypothermia by swimming individually or with the boat to shore. Always stick together. When and if someone does come to rescue you in a motorboat, rounding everyone up will be only more difficult if someone swims off. There is also the risk that an oarsman swimming alone might drown or be run over by a launch.

In one actual incident, an oarsman drowned in an attempt to swim to shore after leaving his swamped boat despite being told to stay put by his teammates. The water was very cold and he seemed to be confused due to the onset of hypothermia. Distances on the water are deceptive. Even if the water is not cold enough to be a risk for hypothermia, swimming to shore may tire someone out. Just because someone can row on top of the water for long distances does not mean that he can swim in it for long distances. Swimming a mile is not equal to running a mile.

In another incident in a large American city, a team decided to row at the very first part of the spring season even before the docks had been put back in after the winter break. After wading the boats in to launch them followed by a bit of practice, the weather conditions became rough as the forecast had indicated and several boats were trapped out on the water. One eight was split in half. (see **Figures 3.1 and 3.2**) Several oarsmen went to the hospital with mild hypothermia after they were rescued by the police. The team stuck together until the police boat arrived. The incident made the local news with video footage. A big question one must ask is why was the team was out on the water to begin with. It was before the docks had even been put back in. What's the rush? Row only when it's safe, not when you're tired of winter on land training.

If a shell or powerboat hits you, do not be concerned about the equipment. Equipment is always replaceable; your teammates are not. Get any injured teammates to shore immediately. This can be done either by using someone's launch or having everyone else row the damaged boat to shore. Leave the discussion of who caused the accident to later. Just be sure to remember who it was that hit you.

 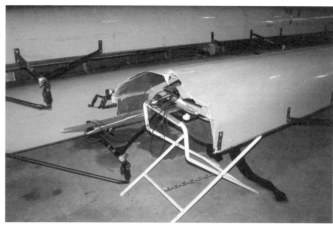

Figure 3.1 Rowing when one shouldn't be ...　　**Figure 3.2** ... creates a new sectional eight that can't be put back together.

Rowing has been described as one of the best low-impact aerobic sports along with swimming and cross country skiing. It is a team sport and your teammates are relying upon you to watch out for potential trouble on the river and to use common sense when facing bad weather. Safety should always be in the back of your mind whether you are practicing or racing. The fastest teams in rowing are not decided by who practiced in the worst weather, but by showing up at the starting line on race day and winning. A team whose coxswain did not use common sense by pushing the limit one day will not be at the line on race day due to equipment damage or worse - teammate injuries. If you like injuries, try out for football. As the bumper stickers say, "Real athletes row, others just play games." Play it smart in rowing, and the only incident you will probably ever have will be an occasional swamping.

Chapter Four

Terms

Rowing has its own terminology which must be learned in order to communicate effectively. Even words such as left and right are different in "crew talk." These rowing terms are listed below in **boldface** followed by their definition(s). <u>Underlined</u> terms are those which you should know within the first week or two on the water as they are essential for you to communicate. Terms that are not underlined can be memorized afterwards, preferably a few weeks thereafter. If a definition includes a term that is defined elsewhere in this list, that term is also in bold face. As stated in the preface, the first usage of one of the following terms in this book is signified by bold type. Please note that every team uses a few terms that do vary from these. In these cases, use the team's preferred words to avoid confusion.

Oarsmen are numbered in order from bow to stern. The oarsman closest to the bow is called the bowman rather than the one-man; the oarsman closest to the stern is called the strokeman. The term coxswain originates from the naval term for the person in charge of a small boat.

A

Aerobic • A stage of a workout when all of the body's need for oxygen is met by what is being inhaled and what is stored in the body. This stage can continue for some time. Weight circuits are an aerobic workout.

Alden • A manufacturer of shells designed to provide a very stable platform for either learning how to row or rowing in rough water. This wide hull design is raced at some regattas in its own category.

Anaerobic • A stage of a workout when all of the body's need for oxygen is not met by what is being inhaled nor by what is already stored in the body. This stage cannot continue for too long. Too much **lactic acid** will be produced that the body will quickly be in pain. A series of short running sprints is an anaerobic workout.

Aligner • A race official responsible for aligning the crews so that all the **bowballs** are the same distance from the finish line. A raised white flag signifies alignment. A race cannot be started until all boats are properly aligned. At races with **stakeboats** or **starting docks**, the people holding the boats will work with the aligner for positioning. At races wherewith no starting docks or stakeboats, the aligner will work directly with you.

B

Back door • A type of **seat race** where the oarsmen do not directly seat race each other in one race following the next. See Chapter Seventeen, Seat Racing.

<u>**Backsplash**</u> • The water thrown towards the **bow** at the **catch**. Too little or no backsplash indicates that an

Terms

oarsman is rowing his **blade** into the water. Too much backsplash indicates too early of a hand lift or a slow change in direction of the blade, which will slow the boat down and cause a jerking feeling at the catch.

Backstay • Part of a **rigger**. A backstay is the angled bar which is closest to the **bow**. Most backstays are adjustable to change the **pitch** of the **oarlock**. See Chapter Eighteen, Rigging.

Backstops • The end of the **slide** nearest the **bow**. Technically, the plastic or wooden stops at the end of the slide which prevent the **seat** from rolling off the slide.

Bailer • A device to empty water from the boat.

Barge • A wide stable boat for training novices. Barges allow a coach and coxswain to stand next to oarsmen to explain technique to them without being concerned about the set. Coxswains learn very little about steering in barges, but do learn about the motions of the stroke. (see **Figure 2.4**)

Beaver tail • A term used for a very large stern rudder on an older wooden shell.

Benchpulls • A common weight circuit exercise to strengthen the arms to assist the **finish** of the stroke. Benchpulls are done lying on a high wooden bench with the weight bar underneath. Proper benchpulls require that the bar touch the underside of the weight bench at the highest point of the lift and that the arms are fully extended when the bar is at its lowest point.

Black tape • Electrical tape used to adjust the **pitch** of the **blade** by wrapping bands of it around the top or bottom of the **oarlock**. Coxswains should always have a roll or two with them in their toolbag.

Blade • The surface on the end of an **oar**. Also called the spoon. Most blades are symmetrical - the shape of the blade on each side of the **stem** is the same, though some newer blade designs are asymmetrical, i.e. the **hatchet** blade. Other blades types include the delta and the modified standard shape.

Boathouse • The storage place for the boats.

Body angle • The term for the angle of the body off perpendicular to the water. A proper body angle is approximately 15% at the **finish**. This term also applies to a position in the **stroke** when the body is towards the **stern**, but the knees are still locked down. Rowing with body angle means that you are using your back.

Body prep • The amount of body preparation for the **catch** - arms, shoulders, and back.

Buoy • A marker which defines a course or a certain distance rowed/ to go. Distance buoys are usually placed at every 500 meters or mile. Other buoys may also be located at the end of the **breakage zone** or every few meters on championship courses. They are also used to mark rocks, obstructions, prohibited areas, etc...

Bow • The nautical term for the forward part of the **hull**.

Bowball • A rubber ball attached to the most forward part of the **bow** to protect that boat and others upon impact. A bowball has the same function as a bumper. When a boat with a bowball hits a dock or another boat, damage is prevented or reduced. Bowballs are required safety equipment.

Chapter Four

Bowclip • A clip attached on the **bow** to hold a number for identification in a race. Most races require that boats have bowclips in order to properly display race numbers.

Bowdeck • See **deck**.

Bowman • The oarsman in the most forward seat in the boat. In coxless boats, he is responsible for steering and watching for obstructions by turning around occasionally. Since bowmen are most likely to get hurt in an accident, they typically do not trust coxswain's steering abilities.

Breakage zone • An area measured in meters or seconds during which a race will be re-rowed if a serious breakage occurs in one of the boats racing. **Jumped seats** do not usually qualify as a serious breakage, though sometimes they do if agreed to by the teams beforehand. See Chapter Fourteen, Sprint Racing.

Bucket • A rigging setup so that two **starboard** or **port riggers** are in consecutive order rather than alternating. A bucket-rigged four might have the **bowman's** and **strokeman's** riggers on **port** and the two and three men's riggers on **starboard**. Another term for a bucket-rigged boat is German-rigged.

C

Cadence • See **strokerate**.

Cap • The plastic cover for access holes to the hull **compartments**. Caps must be secured in place during practice to prevent the compartments from filling with water. After practice, caps should be removed to air out the compartments. Some boats have compartments under each seat and thus lots of caps. You are responsible for ensuring that each cap is closed before launching.

Catch • The beginning of a stroke when the blade enters the water. Opposite of the **finish**.

Check • The term for the amount of energy wasted due to improper rowing. Check usually refers to oarsmen reaching the end of the recovery and not starting the drive cleanly or quickly. The result is that the **stern** of the boat will dip into the water due to the momentum of the oarsmen. Check is also a command as in *Check it down,* i.e., drag the water with the blades to slow or stop the boat.

Circuits • An **aerobic** weight lifting routine usually consisting of such exercises as **bench pulls**, squats, sit ups, jumps, and **composites**. For proper aerobic exercise, a circuit is undertaken at less than maximum heart rate for over twenty minutes with short rest periods. Circuits are an integral part of endurance training.

Clip • A metal or plastic clip under each **seat** which holds the seat to the **slide** at all times.

Collar • A plastic fitting around the **shaft** of the **oar** which prevents the oar from sliding through the **oarlock**. Collars can be adjusted to lengthen or shorten the **reach** of the **blade**. It is important that each collar be tight due to the pressures exerted upon it during rowing.

Compartments • The sealed areas of the boat used to counteract the weight of the oarsmen. Located in the **bow** and **stern decks** and sometimes under each seat, compartments are usually accessible through a **cap**. Compartments should be aired out when not in use to prevent rot in older, wooden boats and mildew in newer models. Any visible puddles of water in the compartments is a probable leak and should be checked out immediately. Condensation is not a sign of leakage, but should be dealt with by opening the caps when the boat is in storage to dry out the compartment.

Composites • A lift which exercises all the major muscles used in rowing. The oarsman stands on a raised platform and lifts the weight bar from beneath his ankle up to his shoulders in an overhand position.

Concept II • A rowing equipment manufacturer in Morrisville, VT which manufactures the Concept II **ergometers**, **Dreissigacker** oars, and **oarlocks**. See Chapter Two, Equipment.

Countdown start • A **start** used in windy conditions which uses a verbal countdown by the referee to give the coxswains an equal amount of time to align their boats. The start begins at the end of the countdown even if the teams are not completely aligned or ready.

Cox-Box™ • A product of the **Nielsen-Kellerman Company** which displays **strokerate** information and amplifies sound. This trademarked term is somewhat generic for all sound amplification systems since Nielsen-Kellerman was the first company to manufacture such products. See Chapter Two, Equipment.

Crab • A term for a situation in which the **blade** is not fully **feathered** before leaving the water. This results in the blade being stuck in the water, severely slowing the boat down and throwing off the **set**. This term is from the claim that "a crab grabbed the blade and wouldn't let go."

D

D-hull • A **Vespoli** hull type that was designed by a computer to minimize hydrodynamic (water) drag.

Dash • A short race, usually 500 **meters**.

Deck • The flat upper surface of the ends of the **hull**. Also a distance of measurement, as in "They won by a deck (length)." Most decks of **eights** and **fours** are equal to approximately 2-3 **seats**.

Decklength • A distance of measurement. See **deck**.

Double • A boat with two **scullers**. Doubles do not have coxswains. The symbol for a double is 2-.

Douger • A homemade tool used to loosen and tighten wingnuts on the boat - on the **tracks**, **foot-stretchers**, etc... See Chapter Three, Safety and Personal Equipment for how to make one.

Dreissigacker • See **Concept II**.

Drive • The part of the **stroke** when the **blades** are in the water.

E

Eight • A shell with eight **sweep** oarsmen and one coxswain. The symbol for an eight is 8+.

Empacher • A German brand of usually yellow colored boat often used by very experienced oarsmen.

Chapter Four

Erg • As a noun, short for **ergometer**. As a verb, to train on an ergometer.

Ergometer • A rowing machine used to simulate rowing on land. Most ergometers used by rowing teams today are manufactured by **Concept II**. See Chapter Two, Equipment.

Et vous pret • The French starting commands for *Are you ready?* This command is rarely used. Pronounced et-voo-prey.

F

False start • A **start** of a race in which all boats do not begin rowing at the same time. Most false starts refer to teams that jump the start and begin to row early. A false start can also refer to the more rare occurrence of a crew staying on the starting line after a race has begun. A false start should result in a call back of all crews to the starting line for a re-row. The team that made the false start will be penalized unless there was a legitimate reason for it such as breakage of equipment.

Feather • Opposite of square - a noun and a verb referring to the rotation of the **blade** at the **finish** when the blade is parallel to the surface. Feathering is the actual motion of turning the blade. Feathering in **sweep** boats is accomplished with the inside hand only rolling the **oar handle**. The outside hand has no impact upon feathering except to provide leverage. A common drill is to reduce the feather of the blade (1/4 feather, 1/2 feather, etc...) or to eliminate it all together (square blades). An incomplete feather will result in **wash** at the **finish** and may result in a **crab**. A feathered blade is parallel to the water's surface.

Fin • A triangular or rectangular part of the boat which is underneath the water on the **stern**. A fin keeps the boat on a straight course when the **rudder** is not in use. Bent or missing fins cause extreme steering difficulties. A fin is the most likely part of a boat to be damaged - by hitting something in the water or by dragging it across the edge of the dock. In extreme cases, a fin may be shoved through the hull if a solid object like a submerged rock is hit dead center. **Rudders** are typically located immediately behind to the fin and may actually be a part of the fin connected by a rubber sleeve as on some Schoenbrods.

Finish • The end of the **stroke** when the **blade** is removed from the water. Also the end of a race.

FISA • The Federation of International Rowing Societies, i.e. a collection of national governing bodies such as the US Rowing. Short for Federation Internationale Societe de Aviron.

Flag • A device that referees carry to align boats at the **start**, begin races, warn poorly steered crews, mark the finish line, and signify that a race is under protest. Official referee flags are either white and red. White flags are used to signal alignment of boats at the start and as an all clear symbol. Red flags are used for the start, for warning crews which have drifted out of their lanes, and to signify a race under protest. Flags of other colors, typically orange, are used to mark the **finish**.

Fly and die • A strategy used by teams who feel they have no chance of winning a race. This strategy is to start the race at too high of a **strokerate** and too much pressure with the hope that the oarsmen can hold on to the early lead. See Chapter Fourteen, Sprint Racing.

Flyweight • A rare weight category for the lightest class of oarsmen. One definition is any male who weighs not more than 135 pounds and any female who weighs not more than 100 pounds.

Footboard • The adjustable wooden or plastic board which the **shoes** are attached to. The footboard is a part of a **footstretcher**, though the terms are sometimes used interchangeably.

Footstretcher • The parts which attach the **shoes** to the boat, including the **footboard**, the adjustable metal bars, and the wingnuts which secure it to the boat.

Foresplash • The water thrown towards the **stern** at the **catch**. Too much foresplash indicates that the **blade** is being rowed into the water wasting energy and throwing off the set.

Forestay • The angled part of a **rigger** leading from the **oarlock** towards the **stern** of the boat where it is bolted onto the **hull** near that oarsman's feet. A forestay is not part of every rigger as some riggers only have a **mainstay** and **backstay**.

Four • A shell with four **sweep** oarsmen. The two types of fours are four with [cox] (4+) and four without [cox] (4-). A **quad** (4X) is a scull boat which uses the same hull as a 4-, but different **riggers**. A four with [cox] converted to a quad with [cox] is a rare boat and is used primarily for training scullers. Its symbol is 4X+.

Front loader • A hull design with the coxswain in the front in a lie-down position.

Frontstops • The end of the **slide** nearest the **stern**. Technically, the plastic or wooden stops at the end of the **tracks** which prevent the seat from rolling off the slide.

G

Gate • A metal or plastic bar incorporated into an **oarlock** which swings up to allow removal or insertion of an **oar**. Gates should be kept tight to prevent oars from popping out.

German rig • See **bucket**.

Gunwale • The edge of the **hull**. There is usually a small lip on the gunwales to reduce the amount of water which splashes into the hull. Often misspelled as gunnel.

H

Handle • See **oar handle**.

Hang • A pause at the catch so that the blade seems to hang in the air.

Hatchet • A new design of **blade** which has a shape similar to a hatchet. This latest design is believed to provide more power in certain conditions than the older designs of blades. See **Figure 2.3**.

Heart rate • See **pulse**.

Heavyweight • A category of oarsmen which is an unlimited weight class. All oarsmen who do not fit into other classes such as **lightweight** and **flyweight** must row in this category. However, anyone including lightweights and flyweights can row in this category.

Chapter Four

Height • The distance between the bottom of the **oarlock** and the **seat**. Extra height increases the distance an oarsman must keep the **oar handle** above the seat to keep the **blade** fully buried in the water.

Height stick • See **rigger stick**.

Hull • The skin of the boat which is in direct contact with the water. The hull is typically made of carbon fiber, fiberglass, wood, or a combination of these. Since the hull supports the weight of everyone on the water, the hull in most boats is rigid and fragile and should not be stepped onto when getting into or out of the boat. Any obstruction in the water can puncture the hull, cause sinkings and make coaches highly annoyed.

I & J

Inboard • The distance from the **pin** to the end of the **oar handle**. See Chapter Eighteen, Rigging.

Jumped seat • The term for an oarsman slipping off his **seat** while rowing. This event <u>is not</u> usually cause for stoppage of a race if it occurs within the **breakage zone**. See **jumped slide**.

Jumped slide • The term for a **seat** coming off the **slide**. This event may, but not always, be cause for stoppage of a race if it occurs within the **breakage zone**. See **jumped seat**.

K

Kaschper • A Canadian brand of shell.

Keel • The backbone of the boat running down the center of the **hull** to which the **ribs** attach. Not all boats have keels since the skin can be manufactured to be strong enough to support all of the weight of the boat. This term is sometimes used to improperly identify the **fin**.

Kilogram • A metric measurement of weight equal to 2.2 pounds. Olympic coxswains must weigh or carry sand to be at least 50 kilograms or 111 pounds. The collegiate weight of 125 pounds is equal to 56.8 kilograms.

L

Lactic acid • A waste product of muscle usage which builds up in the body and inhibits performance. In **aerobic** states, lactic acid is washed out of the body without inhibiting the oarsmen. In **anaerobic** states, the lactic acid is not drained from the blood as fast as it is produced in the muscles.

Lane marker • A marker which hangs above the course or is located after the finish line providing a **target** for a coxswain to steer towards and a way to identify the numbers of the lanes.

Lateral pressure • Pressure exerted upon the **oarlock** by the **oar**. This pressure originates from the oarsmen and helps keep the boat **set**. Lateral pressure is exerted by the oarsmen's inner hand.

Launch • A small motorboat used to carry the coach, spare parts, safety equipment and spare oarsmen.

Lightweight • A weight category for oarsmen. In college it usually refers to males who weigh not more than 165 pounds and females who weigh not more than 135 pounds. Sometimes referred to as midweight.

Lunge • A sudden lean of the upper body into the rigger before the catch, rather than a desired slow lean into the rigger. A lunge will not only cause set problems, but can also cause catch timing problems.

M & N

Mainstay • The center bar(s) of a **rigger**. The mainstay is usually not adjustable in any way, though the **pin** is. The **oarlock** is attached to the mainstay via the pin, along with the **backstay** and **forestay.** See Chapter Eighteen, Rigging.

Megaphone • A device for amplifying sound. Electronic megaphones, such as those manufactured by **Nielsen-Kellerman** - **Cox-Boxes**™ and **PaceCoaches®**, are used by coxswains to amplify their voices. Non-electronic megaphones can be carried or strapped onto the head. See Chapter Two, Equipment.

Meter • A metric term of measurement equivalent to just over a yard, approximately thirty nine inches.

Midweight • See **lightweight**.

Nielsen-Kellerman • A manufacturer of electronic systems for coaches and coxswains. See Chapter Two, Equipment.

O

Oar • Though the oarsmen are the engines of the boat, an oar represents the propeller. An improperly used oar which is out of **pitch** or is not adjusted in some other way can greatly reduce its effectiveness. Oars consist of an **oar handle**, a **shaft**, and a **blade.**

Oar handle • The handle at the end of the **shaft** of the **oar**. Oar handles are usually made of wood and are sometimes covered with rubber, particularly on **sculls**, to assist an oarsman's grip. Newer oar handles are sometimes made of aluminum.

Oarlock • The part which holds an **oar** in place. Oarlocks have a **gate** to open to remove the oar. Oarlocks are held onto the **pin** using a **topnut**. Oarlock **height** and **pitch** can be adjusted.

Oarshaft • See **shaft**.

Octuple • A coxed shell with eight **scullers**. An octuple is a very rare racing category and is used primarily for training. The symbol for an octuple is 8X+. Also called an octoped.

Outboard • The distance between the **pin** and the tip of the **blade**. See Chapter Eighteen, Rigging.

P

PaceCoach® • A display system manufactured by **Nielsen-Kellerman**. See Chapter Two, Equipment.

Pair • A shell with two **sweep** oarsmen. The two types are the pair with [coxswain] (2+ or 2w) and the pair without [coxswain] (2- or 2w/o).

Chapter Four

Pin • The vertical part of the **rigger** attached to the **mainstay** that holds the **oarlock** in place with a **topnut**.

Pitch • Another term for angle. Though it can refer to the angle of the **pin** leaning away from the hull, pitch commonly refers to the angle of the **blade** or **oarlock** off perpendicular while in the oarlock. A zero pitched blade is perfectly parallel to the water on the recovery and perpendicular when square. A five degree pitch indicates that the tip of the blade closest to the **bow** on the recovery is higher than the tip closest to the **stern** by five degrees. A range of three to six degrees is common. Too little pitch results in a blade leaving the water early; too much pitch results in a blade digging deep into the water. Oars can be manufactured with built in pitch. See Chapter Eighteen, Rigging.

Pitchmeter • A device used to measure **pitch** of the **blade** and **oarlocks**. Though it looks confusing, a pitchmeter is easy to use. See Chapter Eighteen, Rigging.

Poagie • A covering to keep oarsmen's hands warm. Poagies cover both the **oar handle** and the hands so that the oarsmen can still directly grip the handle.

Pocock • A brand of boat manufactured in Washington.

Port • The nautical term for left. Also, the term for a sweep **oarsman** on that side, i.e. his **blade** and **rigger** are on that side, usually an even-numbered oarsman. Most boats are **port-rigged**. Opposite of **starboard**.

Port-rigged • A boat **rigged** with the **strokeman** on port side. Opposite of **starboard-rigged**.

Protest • A complaint in a race typically filed by another crew which feels that its performance was hindered by another crew or for some other reason such as obstacles, wash, unclear commands, etc.... A red flag held up by a referee immediately after a race signifies a protest.

Puddle • The result of a **stroke** through the water. A correct stroke should create a whirling puddle with very little **wash** or waves.

Pulse • The number of heart beats per minute. The pulse determines how much a workout is stressing a body.

Q & R

Quad(ruple) • A shell with four scullers in it, 4X. The full name is quadruple. A few training quads have coxswains. The symbol for this boat is 4X+.

Rack • The storage place for boats when not in use. The boat should be stored with the bars of the rack directly beneath the ribs of the hull.

Rate • See **strokerate**.

Reach • The distance an oarsman is able to extend his arm forward at the **catch**. Also the distance towards the **bow** an **oar** can travel at the catch.

Referee • The judge and jury of the race who has the power to eject unsafe or unfair crews if necessary.

Terms

Resolute • A brand of shell manufactured of carbon fiber that is black in color.

Rhythm • The sense that all oarsmen are rowing precisely together so that there is no **check**. A boat with rhythm is more efficient and enjoyable to row.

Rib • The skeleton of the boat. Ribs are made of wood, carbon fiber, or aluminum. Riggers are attached to the **hull** through the ribs. Ribs can be damaged by overtightening of the rigger bolts.

Rigger • The metal or carbon fiber bars that extend from the hull at each seat consisting of a **backstay**, **mainstay**, and occasionally a **forestay**. Riggers are typically bolted onto the boat with 4 or 6 bolts and are made of aluminum, steel, or in more exotic boats, carbon fiber. Attached to the riggers are **oarlocks**, **topnuts**, and **pins**. See Chapter Eighteen, Rigging.

Rigger (person) • A person in a boathouse who is responsible for the maintenance of the boats and the **boathouse**. Only larger programs can afford someone solely dedicated to this important task.

Rigger stick • A straight bar to measure the **height** of the **oarlock**. Also called a height stick.

Rowing (the blade) in • To begin rowing before the blade is completely buried.

Rudder • A small part behind the fin used to turn the boat. A rudder's surface area is only a few square inches, yet properly used, a rudder can handle most turns.

Rudder bar • On all boats, the bar to which the **rudder cables** attach to in order to control the **rudder**. In bow-coxed boats also the bar coxswains use to steer.

Rudder cable • A cable or rope which a coxswain pulls or pushes to turn the **rudder**.

Rudder stem • The long piece of metal attached to a **rudder** used to connect it to the **rudder bar**. The rudder stem extends through the **deck** and **hull** through a small hole.

Rush • As a noun- the motion of arriving at the **catch** too early typically by accelerating into the catch. As a verb - the act of rushing.

S

Scull • As a noun - A boat which has two oars for each oarsman or a sculling oar. As a verb - To row in a boat which is a scull. See also the drill scull it up in Chapter Nine, Drills.

Sculler's catch • A catch which has a very quick rollup.

Seat • The plastic or wooden seat which rests on two **tracks**. Also a measurement of distance almost equal to 4 feet.

Seat racing • A method used by coaches to pick the fastest oarsmen. See Chapter Seventeen, Seat Racing.

Chapter Four

Sectional • A boat which is manufactured in two pieces which allow it to be taken apart for travel. If a team only uses vans to carry their boats, eights must be sectional. The Olympics require sectionals.

Set • The term for the balance of the boat. A boat which leans to one side does not have set. Boats with set move faster through the water and allow oarsmen to row more efficiently than boats without set.

Shaft • The main, long part of the **oar** which connects the **blade** to the **oar handle**. Also called an oarshaft.

Shim • A small wedge placed between the hull and rigger to temporarily lower or raise the height of the oarlock. See Chapter Three, Safety and Personal Equipment and Chapter Eighteen, Basic Rigging.

Shoes • The sneakers or clogs attached to the boat which anchor the oarsmen to the boat. Feet should not be tied too tightly into the shoes to permit easy escape in case the boat flips.

Shooting the tail • Dropping the legs on the first part of the drive without moving any water.

Single • A one-man shell rigged for **sculling**.

Sky • A blade which is too high off the water at the catch.

Skeg • Another term for **fin**.

Slide • The two **tracks** which allow the **seat** to smoothly slide back and forth.

Spin • A verb meaning to make a u-turn.

Sling • A portable rack system to hold boats when no racks are available. Most slings are made of two folding sections of wood or metal with straps between them to hold the boat. Slings must be placed properly to not damage the hull usually at 3 and 7 seat under an eight.

Snap catch • See **sculler's catch**.

Splashguard • A device used to reduce the water that enters boats due to waves. Splashguards are usually part of the boat in the **bow** and along the side of the boat where there is a slight lip along the **gunwales** to prevent small waves from dumping water into the boat. On rough water, this lip is not sufficiently large enough to stop the water and additional splashguards are needed. These can be made of plastic or even tape and attached to the **riggers** to prevent excessive amounts of water from entering the boat and possibly **swamping** it.

Spoon • Same as the **blade**.

Spread • The distance between the center of the **hull** and the **pin**. See Chapter Eighteen, Basic Rigging.

Stadiums • A common workout of running up and down flights of stairs. This is a tough workout that can be dangerous if common sense rules are not followed. See Chapter Twelve, On Land Workouts.

Stakeboat • A small boat in which someone sits to hold your stern at a start. By holding your boat at different points, this person is able to work with the aligner to align the boats.

Terms

Starboard • The nautical term for right. Also the term for an **sweep** oarsman who rows on that side, i.e. has his **blade** and **rigger** on that side, usually an odd-numbered oarsman. Opposite of **port**.

Starboard-rigged • A shell with the **strokeman's rigger** on starboard.

Start • The beginning of a race. Also the first few shortened strokes of a race which get the hull moving at full speed very quickly.

Starter • An official who is responsible for starting the races. He is the official who gives the starting commands, determines if there has been a false start, and in some cases aligns the boats.

Starting dock • A dock used to hold boats at the starting line in order to align the boats exactly and allow coxswains to obtain perfect steering points.

Steady state • A longer type of work out at a pace that does not approach maximum **strokerate** or heart rate.

Stem • Same as **rudder stem**.

Step • The place where one's feet should go when entering a boat. Also, a mini-ladder used to assist the loading of boats on trailers and racks.

Stern • The nautical term for the back of the boat.

Sterncheck • **Check** in the direction of the **stern**. This is more common and disruptive than bowcheck.

Sterndeck • See **deck**.

Stroke • The motion of rowing, as in *Take a stroke*.

Strokeman • The oarsman in the sternmost position. He sets the pace to be followed by everyone. See Chapter Six, Communication Basics and Launching.

Strokemeter • A device used to measure the **strokerate** of the boat. The measurement is usually obtained through the use of a magnet on the bottom of the **strokeman's seat** and a sensor underneath.

Strokerate • The number of strokes per minute. In a race, the average strokerate might vary between 26 for longer races to 38 for short races. The term rate is used interchangeably with rate.

Strokewatch • A handheld electronic device used to measure **strokerates**.

Swamping • A boat filled with water due to waves, rain, or a leak.

Sweep • As an adjective, a boat in which each oarsman has only one **blade**, versus a **scull**. As a noun, a blade.

Swing • The sensation of everyone rowing in synchronization with everyone else so that less effort is needed to propel the boat.

Chapter Four

T

Tanks • An off-the-water training tool typically consisting of a mock-up of a shell next to a tank of water. Tanks either have stationary water in which **blades** are smaller than usual or a pump system for circulating water to more closely approximate rowing on the water. See Chapter Two, Equipment.

Target • A mark on shore or an overhead sign at which a coxswain aims his boat to maintain a correct course.

Toggle • A wooden or plastic handle attached to the **rudder cable** to provide a better grip for the coxswain.

Toolbag • A coxswain's bag to hold various supplies. See Chapter Three, Safety and Personal Equipment.

Topnut • The nut on the top of a **backstay** to hold the **oarlock** between the **mainstay** and backstay. Since a very tight topnut will prevent the oarlock from turning smoothly, topnuts should only be kept slightly more than finger tight, but checked often to ensure that they do not fall off.

Track • A U-shaped piece of metal to keep the wheels of a **seat** following a straight path. Tracks must be kept clean at all times.

Trailer • A truck used to carry equipment to and from races.

U, V, & W

Ultralight • See **flyweight**.

Ultralights (oars) • A lighter class of oars made of graphite to reduce their weight.

Vespoli • A brand of rowing shells manufactured in Connecticut. See Chapter Two, Equipment.

Wash • Water stirred up at the **finish** by the boat as a whole, by an individual oarsman with a sloppy finish, or by the wake of another shell or motorboat.

Washout • The result of a **stroke** by an oarsman who **finishes** by pulling the **oar handle** into his waist.

Watch • See **strokewatch**.

White tape • White athletic tape used by oarsmen to prevent and/or protect blistered hands. Also good for packing up equipment. Do not run out of white tape!

Woodie • See douger.

Chapter Five

Commands

Rowing also has its own list of commands. "Stop" does not exist, only *Weigh enough* and *Let it run*. The commands are listed below in **bold face** followed by their definitions and an example of their use in *italics*. <u>Underlined</u> commands are those which should be learned within the first week or two as they are essential for you to communicate. Commands that are not underlined should be learned afterwards. Please note that every team uses commands different than these below. In these cases, use the team's preferred commands, so that you do not confuse anyone.

Adjust the ratio • Used to correct either a rush or sluggishness on the recovery. The ratio compares the time used by the hands away from the body motion to the slide speed. *Three man to adjust the ratio.*

<u>**Back it (down)**</u> • Row backwards. The blades do not need to be turned around in the oarlocks. *Bow four, back it down.*

<u>**Check (it down)**</u> • Drag the blades on the water to slow and/or stop the boat from moving forward or backward. Having only one side check their blades results in a turn to that side. *Port to check it down, starboard to row.*

<u>**Down and away**</u> • Push the hands down fully at the finish to give the blade more height off the water. *Three-man, down and away.*

Drag (it down) • See **check (it down)**. *All eight to drag it.*

<u>**Early**</u> • A part of a stroke is early. By itself, the word usually refers to the catch timing. *Six-man, you're early.*

Et vous pret? • The French starting command for **are you ready**, (pronounced *et voo prey*). Used with **partez** which means **row**. *Et vous pret, partez.*

<u>**Finish timing**</u> • A reminder to the crew to align their finish times. *Five-man, watch your finish timing.*

<u>**Feather**</u> • Roll the blades to the feather position. *All eight to feather.*

Glide it out • See **let it run**.

<u>**Hands on**</u> • Grab onto the boat and prepare to move it. Interchangeable with **lay hold**. *Hands on.*

Hold water • See **check it down**.

33

Chapter Five

Heads up • Pay attention, something to watch out for is near you. *Heads up, shell coming out.*

Late • A part of the stroke is late. By itself, the term usually refers to the catch timing. *Three, you're late.*

Layback • Go to the layback position. *All eight to layback.*

Lay hold • See **hands on**. *All eight, lay hold.*

Let it glide • See **let it run**. *Bow four, let it glide.*

Let it run • Oarsmen to stop rowing at the finish, hands away, or on the gunwale and allow the boat to glide (run) across the water's surface without the blades touching it. This command is used in some programs interchangeably with **weigh enough**. *All eight, let it run.*

Over the (your) heads • To lift the boat to the over the heads position. *Over the heads, ready, up.*

Paddle • Row at no pressure or to stop the drill/ piece. *All eight, paddle.*

Partez • The French starting command for row, pronounced "par--tay." It follows the French words for are you ready, **Et vous pret**. *Et vous pret, partez.*

Ready all • A starting command used immediately before **row**. *(Sit ready), ready all, row.*

Roll • Two meanings: 1. When out of the water, roll the boat from the waist position to the over the heads position or vice versa. *To the waists, ready, roll.* 2. When on the water, roll the blade.

Shoulders • To lift the boat so that the gunwales of the boat rest on or near the shoulder. *Shoulders, ready, up.*

Sit ready • A starting command used immediately before **row**. *Sit ready, ready all, row* or in some races, *Sit ready, row.*

Square • Make the blade perpendicular to the water. *Square it up.*

Touch it up • Someone to row gently to align or position the boat better. *Bowman to touch it up.*

Three, take two's oar • Three-man to take and row with two-man's oar to turn the boat without pulling the boat forward off a starting dock or stakeboat. *Three, take two's oar for three strokes.* See Chapter Fourteen, Sprint Racing.

Two, take bow's oar • Two-man to take and row with bowman's oar to turn the boat without pulling the boat forward off a starting dock or stakeboat. *Two, take bow's oar for one stroke.* (see **Figure 14.3**)

Weigh enough • Stop whatever you are doing - rowing, a drill, etc... Used interchangeably with **let it run**.

Chapter Six

Communication Basics and Launching

Communication skills are vital for a coxswain. After all, what is the point in knowing everything there is to know about rowing if you cannot effectively communicate this knowledge? It can be very intimidating for a novice coxswain to tell oarsmen whom he just recently met how to row. Unfortunately for coxswains, training sessions do not exist and one is not promoted into the position based upon previous experience. Before worrying about what you should say, you must learn two other basic skills - "How to talk" and "When to talk."

WHO YOU ARE AND WHO YOU ARE NOT

You are a coxswain in charge of your boat. You are responsible for the safe operation of the boat and the well being of your teammates. You must pay attention to errors by oarsmen and obstructions in the water in front of you. You may be a reference source for oarsmen who have questions about technique. You control their actions on the water by telling them when and how to row - all eight, at square blades, etc... You can tell other coxswains that they must move over so you can avoid the rocks. You pass on information from the coach. So far you may have some idea of what you should do.

Coxswains are usually not told what they are not, but I will. You are not the ultimate source of power in the program. You are not a "little Napoleon" with a power trip. As mentioned on the second page of this book, remind yourself occasionally that you as a coxswain have a lot of responsibility, not "power." Do not tell oarsmen to do worthless things, just so you can feel powerful. If you do not like the strokeman's t-shirt, you have no right to tell him to change it. Nor do you tell oarsmen to look you in the eye when you speak. He can hear you just fine. When your bowman is rowing poorly, it is not your responsibility to remind him of this whenever you see him before or after practice whether it is downtown or in math class. You do not tell other coxswains that they should do a certain drill because it works for your boat. It is up to the coach or that coxswain whether to do that drill.

HOW TO TALK

Coxswains need to speak as if there is a high-fidelity sound system in the boat, not a hamburger shop drive-in speaker. Be aware of how you talk. Every nuance in your voice is carried back to the oarsmen. When you are tense or upset, this will carry through to the oarsmen. If you have a very soft, scratchy, or whiny voice, you may not be understood or even liked. No one likes to hear someone talk to them nonstop for two hours without responding. Combine that with a whiny voice and an oarsman will look for another sport. An advantage for female coxswains over males is that their voices do not break during adolescence.

Diction is also important. You are not competing to be heard with anyone else when you are practicing.

Chapter Six

Take the time to speak clearly and slowly so that every oarsman will understand you. A new drill should be explained so clearly and in such detail that the only reason an oarsman messes it up is because his brain is not functioning that day. Anyone with public speaking experience, from a speech and debate club or similar group, will have an edge in this area of diction.

If you find you are confusing your teammates, first make sure that you know what you are talking about. Next, check your speaking speed. Novice coxswains are typically nervous creatures hoping to avoid being caught not knowing something. Talking fast relieves the novice coxswain since he thinks that he is proving his knowledge and worth by saying as much as he can as quickly as possible, so that any mistakes will not be noticed. The last part is true, but it also ensures that everything he says will be ignored. Oarsmen tune out a chatterbox in the stern, just as you tune out background music in shopping malls.

On cold, low humidity days, your voice will likely become irritated. Use a humidifier in your room at night to keep the air moist to soothe your vocal cords. On the water, breathe through your mouth, rather than your nose. Exhale deeply from the back of your throat to force warm moist air over your vocal cords. Inhale slowly to moisten and warm the air in your mouth before it passes over the vocal cords. Eat and drink cold fluids such as ice cream or milk shakes to soothe your sore throat. On days when your voice breaks up constantly, give your vocal cords a rest by saying very little rather than continuing to force words out of your mouth.

WHEN TO TALK

The most important rule of coxswain communication is to not interrupt the coach. It will be many years before what you have to say comes even close to being as knowledgeable as what a coach has to say. The only exception to this rule is if you see something that the coach has not - an approaching boat that you must avoid, or if you know something that he does not - the two-man's slide is broken and that is why he is late or not rowing.

A coxswain's worth and skill are <u>not</u> measured by the amount of noise he makes. If you have nothing worthwhile to say, then be quiet. A great drill to relax the boat and work on the rhythm is to stop talking for several minutes during a workout that is going well. Your command at this point should be, *Let's listen to the sounds of the boat. Stay in time for a quiet row.* Exceptions to keeping your mouth shut during this drill are for an occasional mention of strokerate, time, and/or distance rowed or remaining. As teams improve, a long workout one day might consist of a long **steady state** piece during which you remain silent for virtually the whole piece. However, if a piece is not going well, staying silent only makes the team wonder what you are doing in the stern. They expect you to make the boat row well and give directions accordingly.

Novice coxswains who talk too much can do several things to counteract this problem. One method is to bring along a tape recorder so that you can listen to yourself later. If you find that you are annoying yourself as you listen to the tape later, imagine what the oarsmen must feel. Listen to what you say - how positive is it? How much do you talk? Do you tell someone that he is late and then not return to him several strokes later to tell him if he is on time? Do you tell someone that his rollup is poor, but not describe what makes it poor - timing, skying, etc...? Oarsmen want to improve; otherwise they would not be rowing everyday listening to people criticizing their abilities. You are there to help them improve, not just to criticize. See the section on Feedback From Others later in this chapter for more information on taping yourself.

A second method to counteract the tendency of coxswains to talk too much is to limit your speaking to a specific number of words a minute. This will force you to prioritize what you say. If an oarsman's catch timing is way off, comments about another minor problem are worthless unless you are doing a drill specifically for the other problem. Otherwise, stick to the main problem or two of the day. If a coach came to you and asked you to work on ten different parts of the stroke, you would be confused, as would the oarsmen. Prioritize and minimize what you have to say. Work on the major problems and ignore the minor ones until a later time. An oarsman who gets an "information overload" from his coxswain or coach will tune everything out.

Communication Basics And Launching

WHAT TO SAY
• **Don't say *stroke*, only people who don't know anything about the sport say it.** •

Some of what you say on the water is common to all coxswains - the drills, the commands, and the description of problems. The style of what you say and your specific motivational phrases varies. Much of what you say depends upon you. If you use "street slang" on a regular basis, you are likely do so on the water. Do not think that only four letter words motivate oarsmen. You may cox oarsmen who prefer and expect to hear as much street slang as possible. But for many oarsmen, a continuous stream of street slang is an annoying distraction. Anyone can use street slang; experienced coxswains rely on more than four letter words. If you do use street slang, does your coach tolerate it and is your team motivated by it? You may be surprised to discover that the oarsmen would rather be motivated by something other than what you would not want your mother to hear.

You should never belittle a teammate whether they are in your boat or not directly or indirectly. The two-man does not need to hear that his catch is the worst you have ever seen. He only needs to know that his catch needs to be improved by doing X. Don't say that the two-man's catch is as bad as Jerry's whose catch everyone knows is really bad. It's not professional and is irrelevant to your boat. You may wind up coxing Jerry the next day and he will have heard of your comments.

INTERACTION WITH YOUR COACH
Your interaction with your coach will determine how effective and respected you are, as mentioned in Chapter One, Introduction. When you do talk to your coach, you must be professional and specific in what you say. Any biases you have for or against a teammate should not change your view of his style or abilities. If your coach asks you about the abilities and/or problems of a teammate whom you do not get along with, you must be fair. Otherwise, your credibility is zero and the coach will not listen to your opinions. This also applies to comments about someone you really get along with. A difficult personal decision for a coxswain is telling a coach that your best friend on the team does not belong on your boat, but on a lower level boat. You <u>must</u> be honest not only to yourself, but also to your coach and teammates. This is another reason for not being involved in a boyfriend/girlfriend relationship with a teammate. Your opinions must always be, and perceived to be, fair and honest.

INTERACTION WITH YOUR STROKEMAN
Interaction with your strokeman should be encouraged, but kept private. A good strokeman can often sense things you may not have seen such as a rush from the bow section of the boat. He may come up to you after practice and tell you about the problem. Do more than nod your head. Ask him to be specific so that you understand everything he is saying. People see things from different angles, so ask your strokeman for any drills he feels are appropriate. There may be one you haven't thought of.

When discussing things on the water with the strokeman, keep it private. If you have a microphone, hold your finger over it. The whole boat does not need to hear that you do not know what a particular drill is or you forgot the bowman's name. This interaction should not reach the point where he is telling you what to say and do, unless it is during your first few weeks and you really have no clue as to what is going on. A strokeman is by definition a leader since everyone should follow him. His role is not to be the strongest, swiftest, or best, though he might be. A strokeman's job is to be a steady oarsman who is easy to follow and has one of the best rowing styles in the boat. He should also be somewhat of a "voice" in the boat. A strokeman who occasionally turns around to motivate a team before the race or points out a problem that you may or may not have noticed is desirable.

The issue over which coxswains and strokemen most often disagree is the abilities of each other. The strokeman may not like to hear you tell him that his blade really does **hang** in the air and that everyone else

Chapter Six

is not early. You may not like to hear him tell you what to do constantly or that you steer like a truck. In this case, you may not know what's going on - listen, or he may be a know it all - sit down and talk to him.

If you do have a strokeman whom you feel constantly interrupts or unnecessarily tells you what to do, politely and privately tell him to stay quiet, and continue coxing. If the situation is causing problems and he will be your strokeman for more than a few days, talk to him off the water. In only extremely difficult situations should you take disputes to your coach for a resolution. You might mention it indirectly, but asking your coach to settle this should be a last resort. You are the coxswain - it is your job to talk. The strokeman's job is to row, not talk. End of discussion.

INTERACTION WITH THE OTHER COXSWAINS

Not only are the other coxswains in your team a base of knowledge to draw upon, but they are also competition. This competition can be friendly or brutal depending upon the status of the coxswains in the program and their personalities. The most important point to remember when you interact with the other coxswains in your program is to always be professional. If there is a problem with a boat, piece of equipment, etc..., share this information immediately. There is <u>no</u> reason to conceal this information in an attempt to make yourself look good. If you are practicing with the other boats and see that other coxswains are having problems keeping up with you, slow down so you can practice together. You are a team and you should act that way. Since coaches cannot **seat race** coxswains as they do with oarsmen, a coach will look at more than one skill when deciding who will cox what boat. The competition is on race day, not during practice. Keep this in mind. The rivalry among coxswains should be friendly. Coxswains can have large egos, but the rivalry should never be so fierce that you avoid talking to each other. In the end, it is irrelevant to the team who coxes what boat, just who crosses the line first on race day. The team is more important than you.

FEEDBACK FROM OTHERS

Oarsmen learn through constant feedback from you and your coach. Coxswains must also do the same. If you annoy people on a daily basis by constantly haranguing them, feedback about you will be negative for a good reason - they do not like your style. Your nickname should not be Mr. or Ms. Negative. On the other hand, if you maintain a positive style and receive little or no feedback as a result, do not be satisfied with this. You must receive feedback, both positive and negative. If you do not, you will not improve. It may seem strange to say that oarsmen are lucky to be critiqued constantly for two hours, but in many ways they are. Coxswains are the last to receive feedback from their coach on what they do in the boat because a coach cannot hear what you are saying. Your coach can only comment upon your steering and drill abilities. After each practice, talk to an oarsman whom you feel will give you an honest evaluation for that day's performance. Ask whether your drills were clear, if you spoke too much or explained too little, if you could be heard throughout the practice, etc...? Ask him to tell you at least one positive <u>and</u> one negative thing you did that day.

Some coxswains like to bring along a tape recorder so they can listen to themselves afterwards. This is a great way for you to learn about the way you communicate. Bring a small tape recorder with you and put a plastic freezer bag over it to protect it from water. If you use an electronic amplification system, tape the recording microphone onto the other microphone. Record yourself not only during the piece work, but also during the warm-up and drill part of the workout. When you listen to the tape by yourself later, do so uninterrupted so you get the full effect of the tape. Keep track mentally or in writing how many times you mentioned a particular problem or oarsman. See if you can spot yourself telling someone that their style is wrong without telling them how to correct it, constantly saying the same phrases over and over, focusing on only one oarsman, placing too much reliance on a particular phrase or drill, etc... Then make those changes in the next practice.

Communication Basics And Launching

LAUNCHING COMMANDS

A good example of your communication responsibilities is the launching of the shell. It may sound easy to prepare eight oarsmen and one shell ready for a row, but for a novice coxswain it can be overwhelming. There are other preparations for practice that are discussed later in Chapter Ten, Practicing.

Your first command should be to gather everyone together to prepare to lift the boat from the blocks or rack, *Hands on!* If the boat is heavy, you may need extra people to help carry it. Smaller boats require greater care in carrying since seven oarsmen could carry an eight, but three oarsmen cannot carry a four.

If the boat is upside down on rollers, slide it out by pulling on the rollers, not the hull. Don't pull on the hull directly since you might drag it off the rollers. After rolling the boat out into the center of the aisle, oarsmen who need to go around to the other side should walk around, not over the hull. The boat should <u>never</u> be walked over to prevent its destruction by an oarsman who carelessly slips and falls onto it.

If the boat is upside down on a rack, all eight should reach over or underneath the boat depending on how high the rack is and slowly carry it out. The oarsmen should switch to the correct side one at a time while the other oarsmen hold the boat.

Each oarsman should then countdown from bowman to strokeman when he is ready to lift the boat from the rack or rollers, *Countdown when ready*. When all are ready, repeat the command to lift the shell and then gently lift the boat off the racks, *Hands on, ready, lift*. As the oarsmen lift the boat from the rack, keep the riggers and fin clear of any racks, boats, or obstructions. After the hull clears the rack, push any sliding racks back in, put away blocks, or push the rollers back in. You decide at what height the boat is carried. The easiest height is with the gunwale on or near each oarsman's shoulder, *Shoulders, ready up*. This may not be possible in small areas so the boat may need to be carried at either waist or over the head height, *Waists, ready, down*, or *Over the heads, ready, up*.

If the boat is on slings right side up, the oarsmen should gather on one side of the boat, preferably the side away from obstructions such as other boats that might be hit by your riggers. If possible, the boat should be rolled upside down and then carried at shoulder or waist height. In narrow or low boathouses the boat may have to be carried out before it is rolled upside down.

As you leave a boathouse or storage area, make your presence known to all nearby by yelling out a warning that you are leaving the boathouse, *Shell coming out!* No one should be able to claim they did not see or hear you as they bumped into the shell, throw a frisbee into it, etc... Protect the forward part of the boat by holding onto or walking near the bowball or stern point. Warn the crew of any obstructions nearby or underfoot such as puddles, poles, trees, rocks, sneakers left lying around, etc..., *Heads up for the sneakers on the dock*. New shells are very expensive and you are personally responsible for yours.

Before the boat is rolled into the water, the boat must be lifted to the over-the-heads position, *Over the heads, ready up!* This is commonly done when the shell is carried down the dock or hill next to the water. As the oarsmen walk the boat down the dock, they should begin to slow down to prevent someone from slipping. Remind them verbally or just hold onto a part of the boat tightly so they have no choice. If there are several places to launch from, the preferred place is where the wind, waves, and/or current will push you off the dock as you launch. A crosswind, current, or waves pushing into the dock will pin your boat against it when you need to shove off. It might also damage the boat by bouncing it against the dock, although this will not be the case if you and the bowman do a good job of holding it off the dock.

As the boat is lined up at the water's edge, stand near the fin to protect it from being dragged across the dock as it is lowered into the water. From the over the heads position, roll the boat to the waist position, *To the waists, ready, roll.* (see **Figure 6.1**) Each oarsman should reach into the hull and grab onto a structural piece of the hull such as a rib or deck step. Riggers and shoes are not usually strong enough to grab onto and will be damaged by an oarsman who does. The oarsmen should put their toes on the edge of the dock so that the hull is not placed on the dock by mistake. You should position yourself near the fin so you can protect it

Chapter Six

Figure 6.1 Rolling the boat by holding onto a rib and the hull.

Figure 6.2 Placing the shell in the water with the coxswain standing near the fin. The oarsmen's feet are on the edge of the dock.

Figure 6.3 Placing the oar in the boat.

from being dragged across the dock with a quick push.

From the waist position, place the boat in the water, *Ready, out ...and in.* (see **Figure 6.2**) If the stern gets too close to the edge of the dock, quickly shove it away to prevent the fin from bending or breaking on the dock. Protect the fin at all costs! Fins are designed to break away, but may be shoved through the hull. As the boat sits in the water, you along with the bowman and strokeman should hold the boat off the dock so that it does not rest on the riggers. The other oarsmen should retrieve all of the oars, including the bowman's and strokeman's oars. The two-man should get the bowman's blade, and the seven-man should do the same for the strokeman.

While the oarsmen retrieve their blades and take off their sneakers, use this time to prepare your gear. Plug in the electronic equipment and turn it on, pass out the water bottles if you normally do so, give the **douger** to a person who will need it, etc... Ask any last minute questions now. The oarsmen should put their sneakers in one place on the dock to make retrieval after practice easier. A pile of sneakers will also make it less likely that one will be lost or knocked into the water. If it might rain while you are rowing, sneakers should be placed upside down to help keep them dry. Where theft is a problem, bring the sneakers or at least one of each pair with you.

If the seats to the boat are removed each night after practice, put them in the boat before the oars are placed in the oarlocks. Typically, the more straight edge of a seat faces the stern while the W-shaped edge faces the bow. Next, put the oars on the dock side into the oarlocks. As the remaining oars are put into the oarlocks on the water side, the other oarsmen should hold the boat to prevent it from rolling, *Port to hold, starboard to put blades in,* or vice versa. Oars lying on the dock should be fully extended, but the oars on the water side should be kept pulled in with the oar handles and collars resting on the dock. (see **Figure 6.3**) When everyone is ready, the oars on the water side

Communication Basics and Launching

should then be fully extended and those oarsmen should get into the boat and tie in first, *Port to hold, starboard one foot in ... and down.* There is a specific spot in every boat where oarsmen and coxswains should step. The hull is not one of them! When they are done tying in, the remaining oarsmen on the dock side should then get into the boat and tie in. (see **Figure 6.4**) Shoes should be tied lightly. If the boat were to flip, tight shoes would restrict them from escaping.

Though you can sit in the boat at any time, it helps to get in last when you are rowing with novices to assure that no one has made a blatant error such as an oar or seat put in backwards. After everyone is tied in and you are in the boat, all oarsmen should lean away from the dock to lift the riggers and push off the dock with their hands. You can remain half-standing in your seat and push off with your foot. If the boat is not fully pushed off the dock now (this will usually be the case), use the blades to push off. To prevent the boat from flipping, only half of one side should use their blades to push off the dock further, i.e. only bowman and seven-man (or two-man and strokeman) on an eight. (see **Figure 6.5**)

If a wind or current is holding your boat against the dock, walk the boat down the dock and have bow four row with 1/2 or more pressure as you hop into your seat. Just don't be left behind on the dock by this maneuver. It is embarrassing to see your boat rowing away without you. You can help with a strong push off with your foot that will also prevent your stern point from hitting the dock.

Figure 6.4 Stepping into the boat.

Figure 6.5 Shoving off from the dock with starboard blades.

The entire launching procedure of putting the oars into the oarlocks, tying in, and shoving off should eventually take 60 seconds when there is no one on the dock ahead of you. With more experience, all oarsmen can simultaneously put their oars into the oarlocks and tie in later on the water after shoving off. Fancy crews may even push off with one foot in the boat and one on the dock. Your ability to encourage your oarsmen to launch quickly will be useful on race day where the time and space for launchings and landings are often limited.

Your communication skills are just as important as your knowledge about the sport. And just as your knowledge grows, so do your communication skills. Learn what makes your boat move - it is more than just a drill or command. It is also what and how you communicate. Most important, do not be intimidated by this responsibility or have a huge ego about it. After all, very few people outside the military have the ability to tell a group of people how to move and react for two hours nonstop with very little response. Lucky you.

Chapter Seven

Style Fundamentals

• **Entire books have been written about rowing fundamentals. The small section below highlights the very basics of rowing style. Use your coach, videos, and other resources to gain a more complete knowledge about rowing style.** •

One of your initial responsibilities is to master the fundamentals of rowing so that you can teach them to oarsmen. A coach cannot be everywhere at once and will rely on you to the greatest extent possible. Most novice oarsmen will eventually learn how to row somewhat correctly on their own, but you are there to speed this process along. Every novice thinks that rowing is an easy sport to master since it looks so effortless from afar. A closer look reveals a more challenging task. Every novice must understand the basics- power is unimportant when learning to row, always sit up in a relaxed position, take it slow, if it feels uncomfortable it is probably wrong, and follow the person in front of them.

Since it is easier to teach one individual to row than eight oarsmen simultaneously in an unstable shell. Hopefully, there will be a chance for every oarsman to row several times on an ergometer, in tanks, or on a barge before rowing in a shell. Since few ergometers allow proper demonstration of rolling the blade, only body and slide work can be taught. Placing the ergometers in a straight line will help stress the importance of following the person in front of you.

Before you learn rowing style, learn what the positions in the boat represent. The strokeman of an eight is the leader of the boat with everyone following his rowing style and slide control. The seven-man needs to be as close as a match as possible since this is the basis for starboard and port side timing. They are generally not the physically largest pair of the boat. The largest pair is usually found in the "engine room" of the boat, the middle four. The bow pair represents the balance pair of the boat since they more than anyone else can

Figure 7.1 The finish position.

Style Fundamentals

see the boat lean to one side. They can also see everyone else's blades and can counteract any set problems. They will probably love to tell you where the problems lie within the boat. The bowman in particular will not trust your steering abilities since he will be the one most likely to be hurt in an accident.

There are weight categories in rowing. Lightweight and heavyweight are the two most common. These weight catagories depend upon the league you are racing in. A college lightweight limit is much higher than a high school limit. There is also a difference for male and female weight categories.

• In these pictures, the blades are on the water's surface.
The hand levels should be slightly lower while rowing. •

BODY POSITIONS

Layback and other body positions are difficult to discern from the stern for obvious reason. (see **Figure 7.1**) Sitting up in the boat will help the coxswain see some of these mistakes, but only the body positions of the stern pair will be very visible. At the finish, oarsmen lay back toward the bow with a 10 to 15 degree angle, leaning slightly into the rigger, and sitting up with elbows near the waists. (see **Figures 7.1 and 7.4**) The shoulder angle should match the angle of the buried oar shaft to allow a greater reach. A common error is to lean away from the rigger at the finish to gain more leverage against the oar. If ignored, this incorrect lean will become a permanent part of that oarsman's style and will throw off timing, blade depth, and the set. The hands should be 10 to 12 inches apart. Shoulder movements made by oarsmen should be smooth with no dips or raises. No one should have a "chicken wing" which refers to elbows that are too far away from the body or be "scrunched up" with the elbows too tight to the body. (see **Figure 7.2**) The heads of the oarsmen should be on a level plane with the water. (see **Figure 7.3**) The oarsman's inner hand should exert pressure on the oar to firmly hold the oar collar against the oarlock. This pressure, called **lateral pressure**, helps to maintain set.

Figure 7.2 A back too tense, too scrunched, and just right.

Looking at the oarsmen from the coxswain's seat, you should see only the strokeman and some of the oarsmen behind him. There will almost be a slight gap down the center of the boat as the oarsmen lean into their rigger. (see **Figure 7.1**) At the catch, the oarsmen also lean out of the boat towards their oarlock so that a gap down the middle of the boat appears. This lean helps extend the reach of the blade towards the bow.

FROM THE FINISH POSITION

From a relaxed finish position, oarsmen begin the recovery by rotating their hands

Figure 7.3 Heads too low, too high, and just right.

Chapter Seven

Figure 7.4 The finish position.

Figure 7.5 The hands away position.

Figure 7.6 The body angle position.

down and away from their chest on an even plane so the blades do not wiggle in the air. (see **Figure 7.5**) This rotates the blade out of the water. As the arms become fully extended, the bodies begin to swing forward. Hands pass over the knees before the knees begin to rise. (see **Figure 7.6**) Since the hand levels do not change, the armpits open up. Oarsmen should be sitting up as the body swings forward and the head should not sink down into the shoulders. Where the chin goes, the body will too.

Once the arms are fully extended and the body is almost fully swung forward, the legs begin to compress. (see **Figures 7.7, 7.8, 7.9, and 7.10**) The knees should remain close together. At approximately half slide, the outer arm will be between the knees, and the inner arm will be outside the knees. (see **Figures 7.8 and 7.9**) This allows oarsmen to stretch into their riggers for more reach.

BODY PREPARATION FOR THE DRIVE

Only the inner hand rotates the blade. The oar handle spins through the outside hand. The goal is that the blade rollup is completed at the exact moment the blade enters the water. Since a blade with too little rollup will slice deeply into the water, an early rollup is more preferable than a late one. Most coaches prefer to teach a longer, slower rollup for novices. This rollup time is reduced as oarsmen become more experienced. Eventually, the catch in some teams resembles a **sculler's catch**, which refers to a quick rollup.

As the inside wrist rolls the blade into position, the body compresses into a final, strong position to allow for an explosive drive. The shins should be nearly vertical, but not over vertical. (see **Figures 7.10 and 7.12**) To extend the reach of the blade, the shoulder angle matches the angle of the oar shaft downwards to the water. (see **Figures 7.10 and 7.11**) Since a perfect catch can take years to master, expect that some early catches by novice oarsmen will be rather unforgettable.

Style Fundamentals

As the blade begins to roll up, the height of the hands (and the oar shaft as well) should not change. Only at the end of the rollup should the hands lift into the catch. Since the blade will naturally fall into the water by itself, a major effort is not needed to lower it into the water. The oar handle should be lifted with a quick motion that does not jam the blade too deep into the water. The water should only cover the blade and none of the shaft. If a blade is buried too shallow, the blade will wash out at the finish disrupting the timing and set of the boat and wasting the full energy potential of that oarsman. A deep blade will cause a difficult finish, dragging the boat down to that side.

Figure 7.7 The 1/4 slide position.

The catch involves four separate, but nearly simultaneous motions: (see **Figures 7.10, 7.11, 7.12, and 7.13**)

1. Compressing the body into a tight, but comfortable position
2. Twisting the inside wrist to roll the blade into the catch/ square position
3. Lifting the oar handle while matching the speed of the blade to the speed of the water
4. Quickly changing direction of the slide with an explosive drive

Figure 7.8 The 1/2 slide position.

THE DRIVE

The drive is an exact opposite of the recovery. The legs initiate the drive, not the back or arms. The arms hang onto the oar handle with no attempt at bending the arms or opening the back up made until the legs have almost completed their work since they contain the strongest muscles of the body. The legs are responsible for approximately 70% of the power, the back 20%, and the arms only 10%. As the legs finish their part of the drive, the back joins in. Just as on the recovery, the blade level should be kept steady and the body relaxed with the head up. (see **Figures 7.14 and 7.15**)

As the body finishes, the back swing adds to the speed of the blade through the water.

Figure 7.9 The 3/4 slide position.

Chapter Seven

Figure 7.10 The full slide position.

Figure 7.11 A front view of the catch position.

Figure 7.12 A side view of the catch position.

The power applied on the drive should be continuously accelerating. There should be no fading of pressure toward the end of the drive. As the back swing finishes, the arms join in. The distance the blade travels through the water is extended slightly by leaning into the rigger at the finish. Removing the blade from the water with a quick downward flick of the inside wrist should be effortless to prevent any slowing down of the glide of the hull. The outside wrist should not assist the rolling of the blade to the recovery position except to provide leverage. The result of a stroke should be a swirling puddle with no white water caused by wash at the finish.

The finish involves three nearly simultaneous motions:

1. The tightening of the hands to the body
2. The quick downward flick of the inside wrist to roll the blade
3. A similarly fast down and away motion with the hands

THE BLADE

Since you are unable to see the bodies of the oarsmen behind the strokeman, you must rely upon their blades and blade levels to give you an indication of what the oarsmen are doing. There should be an audible "thunk" at each finish to signify the feather. If the noise is not loud or if several "thunks" are heard, drills for clean finishes and finish timing are needed. An oarsman who has a slow finish will not make a "thunk" when the feather is completed, nor will he be on time.

The blade then follows a path parallel to the water's surface. The blade height off the water should be the same for each oarsman. A high blade signifies that the oarsman's hands (oar handle) are too low. A low blade signifies that the oarsman's hands (oar handle) are too high. Your coach will determine the proper height of the water. Most coaches prefer that novices keep their blades approximately six inches off the water to allow room for mistakes. As teams become more experienced the

Style Fundamentals

blade height off the water is usually reduced to only a few inches. This height will be higher in rough water.

STROKERATE AND SLIDE RATIO
• **The ratio of the slide should be that the recovery takes twice as long as the drive.** •

The strokerate is only a number, yet an important one. There is no single perfect strokerate since it depends upon the individual strength of the team, the rigging, and the distance of the race. A high strokerate will cause a crew to burn out quickly as they expend their energy flying back and forth on the slide, rather than in the water; a low strokerate will not allow a crew to be quick through the water. When rowing with minimal pressure, oarsmen should maintain a strokerate of less than 20. Experienced teams may maintain as high as a 38 during a race, but during short pieces or at the start and finish of a race they may approach 50.

The strokerate can be deceptive and is not the only measure of a crew's slide speed and general effectiveness. To think of the relationship between strokerate, pressure, and slide ratio, remember that it is possible to row at full pressure at a 20 and at a 30, but it is only possible to row at zero pressure while at a 20, not at a 30. Rowing at no pressure at a 30 would require very fast slides, resulting in a poor ratio. The last part of the drive should be the quickest. On the recovery, the speeds reverse - the first part of the recovery, the hands and body angle, are the fastest. Oarsmen then slow down on the recovery as they approach the catch.

Learning the fundamentals of rowing takes time. It is easy to learn the basics within a few weeks. It will take much longer to not only be able to learn the minor parts of technique, but also to be able to spot errors. Watch videotapes of experienced oarsmen and try to spot the flaws in their technique no matter how small they may be. Read magazine articles and books about rowing techniques. And do not be afraid to ask intelligent questions.

Figure 7.13 A side view of an aggressive catch.

Figure 7.14 A side view of the beginning of the back swing.

Figure 7.15 A side view of the end of the back swing.

Chapter Eight

Steering

• Steering in sprint races is covered in Chapter Fourteen, Sprint Racing •
• Steering in head races is covered in Chapter Fifteen, Head Racing •

Steering is the most visible part of a coxswain's job while practicing and racing. You may be the most knowledgeable coxswain in the world, but it will not help your boat's chances in a race if you are steering a course that covers an extra 100 meters. The objective in a race is to take the quickest route from A to B, not a scenic waterway tour. One coach has remarked that the shortest distance between two points is a string, realizing that no one can steer a perfectly straight course. Note that the objective is to steer the quickest route from A to B, not the straightest route. In some cases, the straightest route is not necessarily the fastest since boats can get in your way and choppy areas which you should avoid.

Coxswains must also remember that steering is a constant concern. Cars can be out of alignment due to a wheel problem. Shells can also be "out of alignment" by a side that is stronger than the other. Position of the oarsmen and their strength plays a part in the natural steering tendencies of a boat. A port-rigged boat will naturally turn to port since the starboard oarsmen are furthest forward. A washout by your strokeman will turn the boat towards port, but a washout by your two-man will turn the boat even further towards port.

COXSWAIN VISIBILITY AND POSITION
• While in the boat, act as a part of it - sit still and do not move around •

In the vast majority of boats, the coxswain's seat is in the stern to allow coxswains to see every blade in the boat. Bow-coxed boats are used by experienced teams that do not need as much technical work. In stern-coxed boats, visibility of anything directly in front of you may be obstructed by a low seat, your low height, and/or an extremely tall strokeman. In these situations up to 10% of your forward view may be obstructed. Do not steer a zig zag course to see what is in front of you. You can occasionally look around the strokeman if he is too tall, but do not do this quickly since you will throw the set off. Or sit up in the seat occasionally to look over the strokeman. After a year or two of experience, you will be able to play a mental game of air traffic control to remember when oncoming boats and objects will approach close to you, particularly on your home course. However, there will be times when objects low in the water will not appear until the last second. And there will also be times when the only thing that happens is a sudden noise, a bump, and possibly some damage. It happens even to the best of them.

You can get some idea of who is in front of your boat by looking at the wash around you. If you notice a sharp wave pattern, a motorboat is in front of you. If you cross the waves head on, a motorboat or launch has crossed your path and is not in front of you. If you seem to be rowing in the wave pattern for a while, it is in front of you. Evenly spaced wash or puddles in the water signifies another shell ahead of you.

A coach will often tell you to steer towards a particular target. His reference point is often different since he is usually at a higher point than you and off to the side. Get used to your coach saying, "See that point. What do you mean you don't? It's over there. See it?" If your coach is not clear about where he wants you to steer, do not keep rowing and hope that you will figure it out later. Clarify it now. It is not worth the frustration.

Steering

As you cox your boat, you body position should not sway from side to side. The best way to describe your proper body position is that you are part of the boat. If the boat leans tremendously to port, do not lean away to starboard to counteract the problem. By doing so, you are letting the oarsmen fail their responsibility to hold the boat on keel. They need to know what to do when the set falls off. By moving around in the stern, they have no idea if they have fixed the set or if you did by leaning. The exception to this rule is when turning around a large bend and the rudder is fully turned.

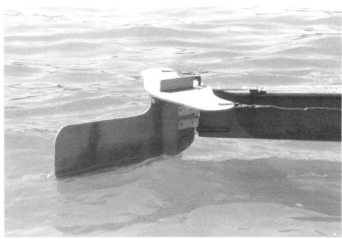

Figure 8.1 An older "beaver tail" rudder.

STEERING FUNDAMENTALS

Coxswains must realize that a shell takes several strokes to respond to the force made by a rudder with only several square inches of surface. Experienced coxswains anticipate turns in order to limit the need for steering and its impact upon the set. The actual force of the rudder depends upon its size, the duration of the turn, and what type of boat it is. A large rudder used on a small boat such as a pair or four will have a much greater effect than a small rudder on a large boat such as an eight. Looking at the narrowness of a shell, it is obvious that leaning out of the boat will cause the set to fall to one side. It may not be as obvious that a turn will also throw off the set. Steering the boat towards port will cause the set to fall to starboard and vice versa. To remember this rule, think of a turning bicycle, car, or sailboat. As the turn gets tighter, the force away from the turn increases.

A turned rudder creates unnecessary water turbulence and drag on the hull in addition to throwing off the set. On most modern boats, a turn should only produce slight turbulence in the water. Excessive turning is unnecessary, slows the boat, and makes the boat harder to control. On older wooden boats with "beaver tail" rudders on the stern, any turn will create substantial wash and disruption of the boat's set. (see **Figure 8.1**) With the exception of rowing on a totally calm lake, shells will always be pushed around by wind and currents. Attempting to control these natural forces can result in over-steering which will leave a visible series of S-turns in the water. These can be easily spotted from above or by looking back at your course.

If you are coxing a boat that is unable to maintain set even on a straight course, it may seem unimportant to minimize the impact of your steering upon the set. Only in your first several months of coxing should you concentrate solely on maintaining a straight course without regard to steering's impact on set. As your steering skills improve along with those of the boat, then focus upon learning how to steer without ruining the set.

WHEN TO STEER

• **Some believe that turning while the blades are out of the water results in less drag and a faster boat than turning during the drive. However, this belief is in error and should be ignored.** •

Approximately three strokes before the turn is needed, gently pull, not yank, on the rudder cable. Steer only when the blades are in the water since a shell is more stable then. There will still be a strain on the set when steering with the blades in the water, but it is much easier for the oarsmen to counteract. Since you will be unable to complete most turns during the short period when the blades are in the water for one stroke, you must turn the rudder repeatedly. It may seem that a lot more effort is needed to turn the rudder back and forth several strokes in a row, rather than just holding it turned continuously for fewer strokes. A continuously turned rudder is more likely to throw off the set and slow the hull speed even further. As you begin to finish the turn, remember the delay involved in turning. Stop using the rudder several strokes before the turn should be completed.

Chapter Eight

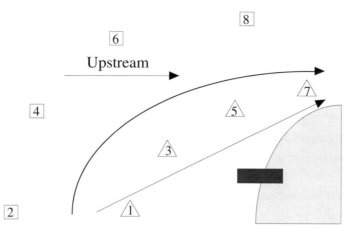

Figure 8.2 What course do you steer?

WHERE TO STEER

When following a shoreline, do not attempt to steer a straight course by remaining a specified distance from shore. Aim for a point in the distance. Very few shorelines are perfectly straight and there may be obstructions which stick out from shore or shallow areas with submerged obstacles. On non-buoyed water stay a reasonable distance off the shore and away from visible rocks. If there are several obstructions or shallow areas on the turn, steer a gradual turn to avoid the obstacle that is furthest away from shore. There is no need to hug the shoreline and constantly worry about steering around the next obstacle. If you attempt to keep a fixed distance off the shore line, you will wind up constantly looking at the shore rather than in front of you.

US Coast Guard markers follow the three R pattern - Red Right Returning. This means that when you are returning from open water towards shore or going upstream, the red buoys or markers will be to your right and the green markers, sometimes black, are to your left. The symbols for red markers is a triangle; the symbols for green (black) markers is the square.

You do not necessarily have to follow these markers since your depth is only a foot or so. These marked areas may be for pleasure boats with a depth of five or more feet or barges with a depth of thirty or more feet. See **Figure 8.2** for possible steering patterns. You could steer between the markers as indicated. However, you should only cut the corner somewhat <u>if you know that there is enough depth there and you have permission from your coach to do so</u>. The area inside the markers might be very deep, particularly near the dock, but there may be a large rock lurking inches beneath the surface next to Marker #7 waiting to rip your fin off. When in doubt, stick to the marked course.

WIND AND CURRENTS

There will rarely be a day so still that you will not have to compensate for winds and currents. Wind and current do not need to be compensated only when both are behind you or are non-existant. Wind is easy to adjust for since you can see it. Current is more challenging to compensate for than wind since current is generally unseen. You may realize that you are being pushed off course by a current only after you are actually off course. The greater the force of the wind/current, the greater adjustment you must make in your course. A wind's/current's speed can be measured just as a shell's speed. To compensate for a cross wind/current, steer into the wind or current as strongly as it pushes against

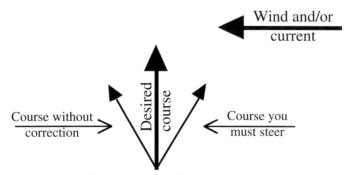

Figure 8.3 The effect of wind and/or current upon your course.

Steering

your hull so that the wind/current pushing against your hull will be cancelled out by the force of your steering. In **Figure 8.3**, the wind/current is coming from the starboard side. If you do not compensate for this force your course will be towards port, represented by the smaller arrow on the left. To adjust for the wind/current, steer towards the wind/current - the small arrow to the right - so that your actual course will be the large center arrow. When the wind and current come from different directions, factor in one of the changes that you must make in your course before determining how you need to compensate for the other force. A 1 knot current will have little impact upon your boat if you are being pushed around by a 15 knot wind.

The only time when it is extremely difficult to handle wind/current is a strong, direct headwind/current. You will find yourself struggling to maintain a very precise straight course as you are forced to starboard and then to port. If you have any choice as to where to steer, maintain a course that does not head directly into a headwind/current. Don't forget that a wind which blows directly against a current will create an enormous chop which should be avoided at all costs.

IS THE RUDDER REALLY STRAIGHT?
• **Since you will eventually steer by the feel of the rudder cables, ensure that any toggles on the rudder cable are spaced the same distance back from the pulleys.** •

You cannot effectively steer until you know when you are actually headed on a straight course. Even if you rotate among five different shells, take the time to find the center point of the rudder cable in each boat and mark it with a piece of tape. Look back at your course to verify if the rudder is really straight. If your course continues to be off to one side continuously and the rudder is straight, the fin may be bent. Ask your coach for assistance.

As you learn how to steer, make the rudder cable tight to have immediate control over the rudder. A loose rudder cable will need to be pushed/pulled further before the rudder begins to turn. If you need to tighten a rudder cable which is made of rope, a quick re-tightening of the rope with a proper knot is all that is needed. Wrap tape around the ends of the rope to prevent future slippage when the rope gets wet. Avoid rudder cables with springs on it by tying a rope around both sides of the spring to bypass the springs. If the rudder cable is made of wire, determine if a way exists to tighten it such as twisting extra wire around a stick. If tightening the wire proves impossible, talk to your coach about the problem and ask to replace the cable with rope. If no spare rope exists, buy it yourself rather than pester your coach. Spend the dollar or two and show your coach that you are determined to change the rudder cable and are willing to do it yourself or at least assist him with it. If your coach is hesitant to replace the cable, tell him that your steering will improve. Just as in other situations, be assertive and know what you are talking about. This aggressiveness will also demonstrate your dedication to improving. However, do not change the cable without asking your coach first.

MAINTAINING A STRAIGHT COURSE
Since the view directly in front of you is often obstructed by the strokeman, pick a point above the his head to steer for. If no such point exists, the best alternative is to either keep your bow equidistant between two points on shore or head towards a target blocked by the strokeman and maintain a course so that you remain unable to see the target. If you are headed out to sea or on a huge lake where the horizon has no distinguishing points, leave the rudder straight and do not steer. As a safety precaution, maintain visual contact with shore at all times. You can also look back at your wash to see if you have been steering a straight course. On flat water you may be able to see up to 1000 meters of puddles. If you tend to oversteer, turn the rudder only a certain number of times per minute to force yourself to plan your turns earlier and complete them more efficiently.

Chapter Eight

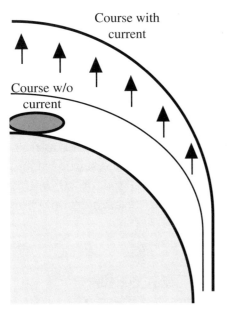

Figure 8.4 How current impacts your course.

DIFFERENCES IN CURRENT

Current is not the same in each location of the river. Although it is more important to remember this in a head race, it does have some impact upon your steering. Current is generally stronger in the center of a river where it is deeper. The shallower areas generally have less current. So if you are rowing downstream, stick to the center of the river for the fastest current. Heading upstream stick to the shoreline.

On a sharp bend, the strongest current will often be at the inside of the bend in the river. Since the river current cannot make as sharp of a turn as your boat, expect to be pushed away from the shoreline on the bend when heading downstream. You should plan on making an even tighter turn than you planned to compensate for the current. (see **Figure 8.4**) Sometimes there will be a slow area right after this bend that collects debris so don't go too close to the shoreline. The usual spot for a debris field is marked on the diagram.

EXECUTING A LARGE TURN

There will be times when you will not be able to complete a turn with the rudder being used only while the blades are in the water. In these cases, warn the crew that you will be making a big turn and hold the rudder almost fully turned throughout the entire turn. Clearly state to which side you will be turning, and remind the oarsmen to hold the boat on keel by adjusting their hand levels, *Entering a hard turn to starboard (port), port (starboard) side to push their hands down, starboard (port) to keep them high.* When a constantly turned rudder by itself will not be enough to complete the turn, have one side also firm up the pressure to assist your turn, *Starboard (port) side to firm it up.* In the very few instances when either of these methods will not work, have one side firm up the pressure and the other side reduce the pressure and/or slide while holding the rudder fully turned, *Entering a large turn, starboard (port) side to firm it up and keep your hands high, port (starboard) side to 3/4 slide and keep your hands down and away.*

During practices, steer a course similar to a race car driver who enters a turn rather wide and then comes extremely close to the edge of the track in the middle of the turn - the bridge or rock in your case, and finishes the turn somewhat wide as well. If you cannot see around the turn completely, steer wide as a safety precaution so that you can see anyone coming towards your boat.

SPINNING YOUR BOAT (MAKING A U-TURN)

• **Whenever you spin your boat, turn into the wind and the current.** •

Turning into the wind/current will maintain your general position on the water. If you turn away from the wind or current, your boat will be pushed downwind and down-current up to 300 meters away from your initial position on the water. Turning a boat around using only the rudder would take a tremendous amount of time and space. Instead, come to a complete stop and have one side drag their blades to turn the boat into the wind/current, *Starboard (port) side to check it down.*

During the first few weeks of practice, use a simple method of spinning the boat. Have only one side spin the boat directly by rowing at 1/4 slide while the other side leaves their blades feathered or buries them square, *Starboard (port) side to hold water, port (starboard) side to row.* This method is less confusing and minimizes the chance that the boat will flip. After gaining more experience, the other side can join in backing down while the first side recovers their blade, *Starboard (port) side to row, port (starboard) side to back it down alternately.* While backing down, blades should not be turned around in the oarlocks. There may be a time

52

Steering

when an oarsman forgets to turn his blade back around to the correct position and has a disastrous effect upon the boat such as ruining the start of a race after backing into the starting platform. There is little additional speed gained by turning the blades around in the oarlocks while turning your boat.

RUNNING OVER AN OBSTRUCTION

• **Never push down an object stuck under your hull since it may come back up through your hull.** •

Your boat will eventually get caught in something. It may be leaves on your fin, rope around a blade, or even worse, something over your bow. This has happened before to coxswains who ran over buoy lines which had large loops of extra line on top. Parts of their bow were ripped off in less than a second. If you pay attention to your course, you are more likely to hit something with your fin than with your blades since you can only see off to the side of the boat. The obstructions that snag an oar will likely fall off without causing damage. In the few case when they will not fall off, an oarsman may have the oar handle ripped out of his hands bending the rigger. You have very little choice but to stop if this happens.

When something wraps around the fin and/or rudder, you will feel a vibration in the stern. You may be able to clear it by quickly reaching under the boat and pulling the debris off while still rowing. If you have snagged a line or other large object on your fin and can't remove it immediately, stop immediately so that it does not rip off your stern. Then reach under the boat and clear it. During the fall when there are many leaves in the cold water, you will become quite proficient at clearing the rudder in a minimal amount of time before your hand freezes.

> For those of you who row in crowded harbors, do not free a stuck winterstick or buoy by pushing it down - it will come back up quickly, possibly through your hull!

When you run a solid object over, it is quite obvious - a loud thunk, a lifting of the hull, a sudden slowing, etc... Solid objects just below the surface - loose rocks, floating oil drums, or tires may be pushed out of the way at impact. If you do hit something that damages the fin, most fins are designed with a weak point on the attachment bolts to break away without going through the hull. If the fin is ripped off, your boat will veer from side to side as you row back home for a replacement. A bent fin should not be repaired on the water since you cannot see it directly and you might cause more damage. A fin which unfortunately did not break away and was pushed through the hull will flood your stern compartment and damage the ribs inside the sterndeck. You must row back home immediately. If there is a launch nearby and your stern is flooded, take out the stern pair so that the stern does not completely sink. You should remain in the boat to steer as best you can and give commands, but you will be halfway underwater. You hit something - you suffer the consequences.

Oarsmen and coaches often feel that steering is an easy job. Steering does not just happen; you learn how to steer. Take the time to learn how to steer when no one really cares - during the first months of the season. When racing season approaches and you need every last tenth of a second to win, it's too late and your team will suffer.

Chapter Nine

Drills

• See the Coxswain's Drill Card for which drills are appropriate for which problem •

There is no master list of rowing drills. Each coach and coxswain develops drills which are useful to his or her program. There are drills which are somewhat common throughout rowing. These common drills are listed below. **Underlined** drills are those which should be learned and used within the first month or two. Drills that are not underlined should be learned afterwards, though six months or more may pass before you use any of them. Since the names used to identify these drills vary from program to program, use the team's preferred terms for the drills, so that you do not confuse anyone

Catch placement drill • A stationary drill focusing on the motions of the catch, recovery slide speeds, and catch timing. While sitting six inches from the catch with blades either squared or feathered, oarsmen work on moving towards the catch in time with the person in front of them, placing their blades in the water with the correct amount of backsplash/foresplash. No actual rowing takes place. The distance from the catch can be increased until the oarsmen begin the drill from the finish.

Catch sequence drill • A moving drill also focusing on set at the catch, the motions of the catch, recovery slide speeds, and catch timing. This five part drill begins with the oarsmen rowing only the first six inches of the slide, increasing to legs only, legs + back, legs + arms, and then regular rowing. Novices should do this drill on the feather with at least one pair setting up the boat. More experienced oarsmen can do this drill with all eight at square blades.

Circular rowing • Blades are recovered with the blades tapping the gunwales after the hands pass over the ankles. The tap should produce a soft noise to synchronize timing. Circular rowing works on set and recovery timing.

Cut the cake drill • Blades feather and recover to either hands away, body angle, 1/4 slide, or 1/2 slide before returning to the finish position a second time and then starting a normal recovery. The height of the blade off the water should be constant throughout the drill and the speed should be the same as they would have been with a normal stroke. By maintaining the same speed, there will be a strong bowcheck during the second recovery. The cut the cake drill works on the set of the first part of the recovery.

Drag and glide • A pair rows for ten strokes with one pair setting up the boat and the remaining four dragging the blades down. Then the same four dragging their blades let it run so that the sensation at the catch changes from a strong resistance to a light resistance. Drag and glide works on quickness off the footboards.

Drills

Exaggerated layback • The body lays back further than usual at the finish to work on body swing and acceleration.

Exaggerated slowness • The strokerate is lowered to 14 or lower on the paddle and 16 or below at full pressure. Exaggerated slowness works on timing and gives the coxswain extra time to spot exactly where problems occur on the recovery as well as identifying those who rush on the recovery.

Eyes closed drill • Rowing (not coxing) with the eyes closed for at least 10 continuous strokes. This drill forces oarsmen to listen to the sounds of the boat and will expose the tendencies of oarsmen to rush which may not occur when they can see what they are actually doing.

Feet untied rowing • Rowing with the feet totally out of the shoes making it difficult to remove the blade from the water with a sloppy finish.

Finish sequence • A variation of the pick drill, pausing every forward body angle for approximately ten strokes. Then, continuous rowing at the same position. After ten more strokes, row at the next step of the pick drill pausing every forward body angle, etc... The finish sequence synchronizes the hands away and body angle speed on the recovery.

Five stroke alternation drill • A variation of the pick drill - five strokes at full slide, then five at 3/4 slide, all the way down to quick pick, and then back up to full slide.

Freefall drill • Alternate rowing one stroke at 1/4 slide, then one stroke at full slide. This drill highlights any tendency to rush in the boat and emphasizes the contrast between the beginning and end of the recovery.

Gunwale high rowing • Blades are recovered so that the blades are the same height as the gunwales - about six inches off the water. Gunwale high rowing works on blade height and the lifting motions of the catch.

Inside arm only • Rowing with the outside arm behind the back. This drill focuses on the rolling motions at the finish and catch. A great drill to force oarsmen to not use their outside hand to roll the blade. It also extends the reach at the catch. (see **Figure 9.1**)

Figure 9.1 The inside arm only drill.

Chapter Nine

No blade height • Dragging the blades on the water on the recovery. There is no excuse for the boat being off set when rowing with no blade height since all it will take to correct the set is one side lifting their hands.

Outside arm only • Rowing with the inside arm behind the back - the blade must be squared. The outside arm only drill focuses on the leverage that the outside arm provides and the drawing of the oar handle into the body. (see **Figure 9.2**)

Pair joining in drill • At 1/2 pressure, pairs join in rowing ten strokes at a time until all are rowing. This drill should be alternated so that each pair starts the drill once. This drill highlights the increase in boat speed as each pair of oarsmen joins in.

Pause drills (every X strokes) • Pausing every one to five strokes at the finish, hands away, forward body angle, 1/4 side, 1/2 slide, and 3/4 slide positions. Pause drills work on set, timing, and slide control.

Pause every catch • Blades drag on the water on the recovery and pause flat at the catch. The time between pauses is slowly reduced to near continuous rowing - a variation of pause drills. This drill focuses on catch set and timing.

Pick drill • This drill begins at reduced slide rowing at quick pick - arms only, swing pick - arms and body angle, followed by rowing at 1/4, 1/2, 3/4, and full slide. This extremely basic drill is one of the most common. The pick drill is used for warm-ups as well as working on individual parts of the stroke.

Reduced feather drills • Rowing with reduced feather, usually 1/4 or 1/2 feather. This drill is an easier version of the **square blade drill** and forces oarsmen to control their feathering more precisely.

Rowing in the air • Taking a stroke with the blades in the air. This drill is for experienced crews and should not be done more than every fourth stroke to allow the boat to maintain its speed. Rowing in the air is more of a challenge than anything else to keep the boat in time and on keel when the air stroke is made.

Russian drill • A drill for experienced oarsmen in which the number of oarsmen rowing and the slide length varies. The drill starts off at 1/4 slide with all eight rowing. After ten strokes, bow four drop out by gunwaling

Figure 9.2 The outside arm only drill.

Drills

their blades for ten strokes. All eight row again for ten more strokes, then another four drops out by gunwaling their blades. After all combinations of oarsmen have completed the drill, the slide length is reduced incrementally to quick pick and then back up to full slide. This drill forces oarsmen to row as perfectly as they can since it magnifies any problems by throwing the set off. Use this drill to spot a problem pair.

Scull it up • Reducing the slide length while increasing the strokerate and pressure. Eventually the oarsmen will be rowing at full pressure, 1/4 slide, and at a high strokerate up to 50+. Sculling it up works on quickness of all parts of the stroke and is best used no more than twice immediately before a start and/or race.

Square blade drill • Rowing with no feather. This drill makes it easier to finish and for the coxswain to spot hand level problems.

Stationary catch drills • See **catch placement drill**.

Stationary finish drills • With the boat at a dead stop, blades flick out of the water together with the slide increasing incrementally up to 1/2 slide. Stationary finish drills work on clean finishes and recovery timing.

Straight arm rowing • Rowing with straight arms so that the arms do not break at the finish - part of the **catch sequence drill**. Straight arm rowing focuses on the hang of the body on the oar handle and prevents anyone from breaking their arms before the back swings.

Wide grip drill • Rowing with the inside hand gripping the shaft of the oar rather than the oar handle. The wide grip drill forces oarsmen to lean into the rigger at the catch.

0% to 50% pressure (also 25% to 75% and 50% to 100%) • Rowing with 0% pressure at the catch with a continuous acceleration to 50% pressure at the finish. This drill highlights the need to accelerate the drive by swinging the back and zipping the arms into the body preventing oarsmen from fading at the finish.

1,2,3 set (stationary) drill • At any point on the recovery with the blades buried, on your command "1" starboard side lowers their hands; on "2" port side lowers their hands; and on "3" both sides even out their hands. This is a very basic set drill which reinforces the point that hand levels impact upon the set.

1,2,3 rowing drill • From the finish on your command "1" blades are feathered and recovered to hands away; on "2" further recovery to body angle; and on "3" blades are rowed through the water pausing at the finish. This drill focuses on basic recovery timing and body positioning.

Chapter Ten

Practicing

Unlike races that are exciting no matter what happens, practices are by nature very boring. The goal is to row the same stroke over and over until everyone in your boat masters technique and timing. You must keep practices interesting and worthwhile. Following a pattern of the same drills every day is extremely boring and will quickly lead you nowhere. There are drills that should be done every day - the pick drill, any basic catch drill, and any basic finish drill. Other drills should vary, depending on the needs of the team. Though your coach will provide you with a list of needed drills, feel free to add necessary drills, but only when the coach feels you should not be doing something else.

GETTING READY

Just as preparation for a race is important, so is preparation for a practice. Although your coach is in charge, help him out by making sure the oarsmen you will cox are there. Rowing with seven oarsmen, instead of eight, is a great way to waste a day. If shove time is at 3:30, then be ready to launch ten or fifteen minutes before hand to handle any last minute problems. Ensure that any equipment problems from yesterday are fixed, rather than forgotten. Check the weather to decide what part of your practice area you should train on and if splashguards would be helpful. Write the lineup and workout on your Coxswain's Drill Card. If you have never met your three-man before, introduce yourself and learn what name he responds to. If there are four Chris's in the boat, you will have to use more than just first names. Last names and nicknames work just as well. Don't use the numbers of their seats - you don't like "Hey, coxswain." Everyone has a name. Use them.

Make your equipment bag available to the oarsmen. Oarsmen should tape up their hands with white athletic tape before launching if they usually do so. If an oarsman needs to shim up his rigger, see if this can be done on the rack before launching. If there is water available for your water bottles from where you launch

Figure 10.1 Does this look familiar?

Practicing

and you are responsible for this task, fill up there after rinsing the bottles out once or twice. No one likes slimy water or the stomach problems caused by that water. If the water comes from a hose, let the water run a bit before filling the bottle. This eliminates the possibility of contamination in the hose and avoids the unpleasant vinyl hose taste. Most oarsmen will stretch or run before practice on their own. If the practice is early in the morning or on a cold day, hold a mandatory time for stretching followed by a light run for a few minutes. You should go along on a warmup run too, since it will wake you up mentally and demonstrate your commitment to the team.

> **FOR LAUNCHING SEE PAGES 38 TO 40**

THE WARMUP

A common warmup begins with two or four oarsmen setting up the boat and the remaining oarsmen rowing the pick drill. This drill should rotate through the boat - bow four, inner four, stern four, bow six, stern six, and then all eight. The pick drill should set the tone for practice that day. Since the pick drill starts with an extremely short stroke - arms only, demand excellence from the beginning. If someone is late at the catch now, he will probably be so at 3/4 slide. Eventually as boats improve, the pick drill can be shortened to all eight immediately after clearing the dock.

Your coach will tell you most the drills to be accomplished that day. Your initiative on the water is usually appreciated. If another boat needs to catch up to you, do stationary drills such as stationary finish drills to pass the time. Sitting still accomplishes nothing and can lead to wandering minds that take several minutes to re-focus on rowing. In cold weather, use stationary and semi-stationary drills sparingly to prevent the team from becoming cold. If these drills need to be prolonged in cold weather, do them at the beginning of the practice when the layers of clothes are still on or allow your teammates a few moments to put some layers back on.

After the drill part of the warmup is accomplished, several minutes of rowing at a steady state pressure will physically warmup the team. If short piece work is the focus of the practice, do some ten and twenty stroke pieces after the steady state. The strokerate of the first ten should be in the high teens or low twenties. The last warmup ten or twenty should be at or above the strokerate you intend to row at during the pieces. If longer duration pieces are the focus of the day, do not waste your time rowing high strokerate pieces during the warmup unless the crew is sluggish and asleep.

GENERAL COMMENTS ABOUT PRACTICE

Each practice is different in terms of what needs to be worked on that day. Oarsmen who have had major difficulty with a specific motion will still have that problem until it slowly goes away with your constant attention and correction. However, oarsmen have minor problems that can appear and disappear daily. An oarsman distracted by something on land - a test, bad day at work, etc... will have extreme difficulty keeping time and staying focused. Your job is to reduce these distractions by staying upbeat and focusing on rowing.

High expectations are the best way to maintain focus. From the first minutes on the water, do not allow poor rowing to occur without your attention. If the three man's catch is late, tell him that info and why immediately, *John, your hands are too slow away from the body and you're late at the catch.* Within a few strokes, tell him if he is still late, has improved slightly, or is on time. Do not frustrate oarsmen by not telling them if they have improved. Always be specific when you praise or criticize an oarsman's style. Comments such as *John, watch your timing* are meaningless unless the oarsman knows specifically what his problem is. If John often pushes his hands away from his body too slowly and is late as a result, he will know what you have implied by saying, *Watch your hands away.* Otherwise always state what the problem and the solution are. The phrase "If you're not part of the solution, you're part of the problem" applies here as well. Never just say something; say something useful.

Chapter Ten

Figure 10.2 A few problems on port side - height, four-man's bent arms as he catches early, and the wash under the strokeman's blade.

There will be times when the rhythm of the boat will be thrown off by a distraction on the water or on shore. Quickly correct the disruption within one or two strokes, *Heads in the boat, let's focus on us not the windsurfer.* You do not need to be a scrooge about it though. If you want to look at it, so will they. The fact that you almost ran over a windsurfer will distract them no matter what you say. Handle distractions caused by large waves in the same manner, though they are a safety concern. See Chapter Three, Safety and Personal Equipment.

If your boat is not rowing well, emphasize drills that work on the problem. (See your Coxswain's Drill Card for ideas) If you cannot remember a good drill, ask your strokeman or seven-man without letting everyone else on the boat hear. He will undoubtedly have something to say. Do not frustrate the boat by continuing a drill that is not working. Instead, move on to another drill. When the boat is just frustrated or tired and will not respond to your words or drills, stop the drills and take a water break. If poor rowing occurs in the middle of a piece when drills or stopping for a water break is not an option, encourage the boat to relax and adjust the slide ratio, *Let's relax on the recovery. Breathe it out by sitting up and keeping the shoulders relaxed.* Only in a worst case scenario should you consider ending a workout early and this should only happen once or twice a year.

> Never scream *Relax* in an attempt to calm a tense boat. This will only have the opposite result since your voice carries what you feel. I did this in high school and it wasn't appreciated. Don't forget that sometimes coxswains are the ones making their boats tense.

PRACTICE AS IT RELATES TO RACING

Oarsmen train almost every day to prepare physically for a few minutes of racing each year. Novice oarsmen and coxswains are at a psychological disadvantage during their early races. Fear and/or uncertainty in a race can result in the ignorance of such basics as steering, timing, etc... To counteract this fear of the unknown, coaches create equal boats to train and race against each other. This permits balanced racing and an element of the unknown so that one boat does not always beat the other boats.

After several races, most oarsmen will become used to racing and not fear it as much. One of your jobs as a coxswain is to make race days just like any other practice day, except that there is only one piece to be rowed. Preparing for a race must begin during practices well before race day. During each practice that involves piece type workouts against another boat, remind the boat of its similarity to racing by calling that practice as you would a race.

Within three or four weeks of your first race, begin to remind the boat occasionally of the importance of each stroke. If your boat cannot row consistently well in practice, it is doubtful that it will in a race. You must emphasize and the oarsmen must expect that every stroke improve until it reaches perfection. Since concentration is usually better when there is another boat or two nearby to pace oneself, the coach will keep his boats together. With only one boat, there is a tendency to mentally fall asleep if a coxswain is not paying attention to errors that should be corrected.

Practicing

WHAT TO LOOK FOR IN PRACTICE

• Drills recommended to correct a particular problem are listed in boldface type. •
• Problems with technique are listed below along with the most important drills
to use to correct the problem. See your Coxswain's Drill Card for a list of drills
for a particular problem. Definitions of drills are listed in Chapter Nine, Drills. •

BOAT SET

The boat must be balanced so the oarsmen can row from a level position. The term **set** refers to the balance of the boat. If a boat is not set, a boat will move slower through the water not only due to increased friction of the water upon the hull, but also due to oarsmen who are unable to apply their power effectively. A boat that is not set is <u>extremely</u> frustrating to row and cox in. Hands will be smashed against the gunwales, oarsmen will wash out or dig depending on what side they are on, etc... You must correct the set of the boat whenever it falls off. As your crew becomes more experienced, the oarsmen may instinctively correct the set without further instruction by you. Novice crews, on the other hand, will require many reminders about the set. Unfortunately, almost everything oarsmen and you do can throw off the set. Even poor rigging can disrupt the set. A single oarsman doing any of the following can throw off the set:

- Catching late or early (see **Figures 10.4 and 10.17**)
- Finishing late or early (see **Figure 10.18**)
- Rowing the blade into the water (see **Figure 10.11**)
- Rowing with the blade too shallow/ deep (see **Figures 10.7, 10.8, and 10.9**)
- Washing out or dumping at the finish (see **Figure 10.9**)
- Leaning improperly into the rigger at the finish and catch (see **Figures 10.15 and 10.16**)
- Rolling the blade at the wrong time (a small effect) (see **Figure 10.5**)
- Tilting knees to one side
- Failing to use enough lateral pressure or foot pressure
- Looking out of the boat

Don't think that oarsmen are the only ones who throw off the set. Coxswains can also disrupt the set by doing any of the following: (some of which are unavoidable)

- Steering when the blades are out of the water (a large effect)
- Steering when the blades are in the water (a small effect)
- Leaning to one side

In **Figure 10.3**, the set has dipped greatly to starboard on the recovery. Starboard side hands are almost touching the gunwales, while port side hands are far above the gunwales. The simple solution would be for starboard side to raise their hands (oar handles) on the recovery and for port side to lower theirs. If the oarsmen need a reminder of the basics of set, stop the boat and do the **catch placement drill** and the **1,2,3 set drill**. Since virtually everything that an oarsman has an impact upon the set, there are a large number of drills that you can use to improve the set of your boat. Drills to work on set in general include **pause drills** and the **exaggerated slowness drill** both to

Figure 10.3 The set dips to starboard - note port hand levels are higher than starboard and the starboard blades are dragging on the water.

Chapter Ten

pinpoint the place where the set goes off, and the **pick drill**.

Oarsmen can correct the set with their feet and the lateral pressure of their hands. In **Figure 10.3** the set could have been helped somewhat by port side forcefully pushing their oars into the oarlocks. Since lateral pressure is very important to the set, at no point in the stroke should the collars of the oars not be firmly pushed out against the oarlocks. Oarsmen who have a tendency to lean away from their rigger at the finish will often pull their oar out of the oarlock. **Stationary finish drills** can help this problem. For fine tuning the set, all of the oarsmen pushing down their right foot (and your left foot) and raising their left foot (and your right foot) would help to balance the boat. In **Figure 10.3** it is unlikely that only adjusting the feet would have any impact since the hand levels are so clearly off.

Drills to work on set at the catch and on the drive include the **catch sequence** and **catch placement drills**; **pause every catch**; **the inside arm only** and **outside arm only drills** to work on the leverage each arm has on the oar and to pinpoint which arm is causing the set problems; and the **wide grip drill.**

Drills to work on set at the finish and recovery include **stationary finish drills**; the **finish sequence**; **gunwale high rowing** and **no blade height** which makes everyone row at an obvious height off or on the water during the recovery; the **cut the cake drill**; **exaggerated layback drill**; **straight arm rowing**; the **wide grip drill**; and the **freefall drill**.

Drills that do not work on correcting the set directly, but do force oarsmen to pay more attention to it include **circular rowing**; the **eyes closed drill**; the **square blade** and **reduced feather drills**; **five stroke alternation**; and the **Russian drill**.

BLADE TIMING

As you gain experience, your knowledge of timing becomes more specific. In the early stages of an oarsman's development, focus on the timing of the catch. This is the most basic technical requirement of a crew - all of the blades must enter the water simultaneously. (see **Figures 10.2 and 10.4**) This does not mean that you should ignore blatant finish timing problems until the catch timing is perfect. Someone may not be pulling the oar handle all the way into his body or is not lying back properly. As your boat develops, you should begin to focus on finish timing followed by rollup timing, etc... Be specific as to who is late or early. Catch timing is what the terms *early* and *late* generally refer to when there is nothing else to specify it. As oarsmen gain experience, perfect timing includes simultaneously leaving the water, feathering together, rolling up together and synchronizing all parts of the stroke such as hands away, 1/4 slide, 1/2 slide, etc... The most common cause of an early catch is a rush on the recovery. (see **Figures 10.17 and 10.18** and the section on slide control)

Figure 10.4 The bowman is late at the catch, but a near perfect catch by the three-man with a foresplash <u>and</u> a backsplash vs. bowman rowing it in.

If your bowman is late, the seven man may be late and everyone behind him is just following him as they should. Rather than say *Seven man late,* be more specific - *Bow through seven late*. If only two through six are late, then say that. Repeated use of general comments such as *We need to work on timing* are worthless and usually infuriate the oarsmen.

Drills to work on catch timing include **the catch placement drill; the catch sequence; circular rowing** to ensure that the oarsmen are in time in the middle of the recovery from a simultaneous tapping noise; **1,2,3 rowing drill; pairs joining in; pause drills; pause every catch;** and the **pick drill.**

Practicing

The next concern is that all of the blades leave the water simultaneously. Drills to work on finish timing include the **stationary finish drill**; **cut the cake drill**; **exaggerated layback drill**; and **pause drills**. Finish timing problems can lead to complaints by other members of the team that an oarsman is not pulling hard enough, resulting in a late exit from the water. Never allow this conversation to occur. Oarsmen need to be focused on their individual abilities, not the abilities, or lack thereof, of others.

Sometimes other things besides drills are needed to correct catch timing. An oarsman's foot stretchers may be set so far toward the stern that the wheels of the seat hit the end of the slide forcing him to catch early since he cannot compress any more. In the opposite

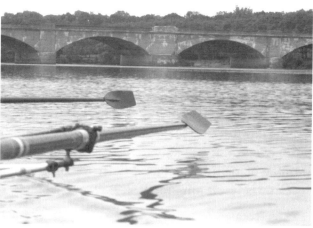

Figure 10.5 Either a late rollup by the three-man or an early rollup by the bowman.

case, an oarsman may have enough room left on the slide that he over-compresses and falls behind in timing. In addition the angle of the footboard may be incorrect making it uncomfortable for an oarsman to compress fully. Rigging can also cause substantial timing problems. An oarsman with long legs and arms will have a longer distance to row through the water than a shorter oarsman. Adjusting the foot stretchers and slide tracks will help adjust for this, but changing the load of the blade is the more thorough solution. Your coach will decide if this is the case, not you. You might mention the problem and your suggestion to him, but never change the rigging without asking your coach first. He will almost always do it himself. See Chapter Eighteen, Basic Rigging.

BLADE ROLLUP

Rollup timing is a very visible part of the recovery. (see **Figure 10.5**) Rollup timing by itself is not very important for novice boats. However, rollup timing is a good indicator of catch timing and the ability of an oarsman to blend his style with the rest of the boat. Rollup timing is a very visible action which is relatively easy to correct, *Four man, delay the rollup slightly* or *Five man, your rollup is about two feet late*. It is common for a rollup to be late, rather than early. Tell the oarsman a specific point that he should begin his rollup, *Six man, your rollup is a bit late. Begin to rollup when your hands pass over your shins.* If he still does not understand, have him watch his rollup for a few strokes. If the oarlock is too tight and restricts the movement of the oar, extra effort may be needed to rollup the oar. Tell you coach and he may loosen the oarlock **topnut**

Figure 10.6 An over-roll at the catch ...

Figure 10.7 ...and the result.

Chapter Ten

or apply lubricant to the oarlock.

Compared to other problems, rollup timing problems are one of the easiest to correct. Drills to work on rollup timing include **inside hand only** for general rollup control - particularly effective if an oarsman incorrectly uses both hands to rollup his blade; the **stationary catch drill**; **pick drill**; **exaggerated slowness drill** to see where oarsmen are early or late on the rollup; **eyes closed** so oarsmen call feel their rollups; and **reduced feather drills**.

Other rollup problems such as an overdone rollup are less common. (see **Figures 10.6 and 10.7**) This is often due to an oarsman who squares his blade with both hands. Remind him to keep his outside wrist straight and have him row at square blades to reinforce the correct blade position. Then slowly increase the feather until the blade fully feathers. Once the oarsman begins to over-roll his blade, tell him so that he can feel what his error is. Tell him a few strokes later if he is rolling his blade correctly.

BLADE HEIGHT

Since blade height affects the set of the boat almost as much as timing, it should be your next concern after blade and rollup timing. Most coaches prefer novices to keep their blades higher off the water than the blades of more experienced oarsmen. This extra height allows room for mistakes and emphasizes the need to lift the entire blade into the water.

Blade height is the exact opposite of hand height, so it may be more helpful to novice oarsmen for you to talk about hand levels rather than blade height. If the height of a blade lowers in the middle of the recovery, an oarsman's knees are rising before the oar handle passes over them. This error will force the oarsman to lift the oar handle above his knees (lower his blade) to clear them, possibly smacking his blade on the water. The oarsman will often return the oar to the correct height after clearing his knees even though he says he never changed the oar height. Be very specific about the problem, *Seven man, watch your hands away blade height. Keep your knees down until after your handle passes over them.* Try **square blades** to force a solution.

Until boats are rigged individually for each person, a tall oarsman may be forced to row in a seat with a rigger set for a shorter person. If these problems are not severe, oarsmen can row with an uncomfortable, modified hand level that will not allow their hands to go down at the finish as far as they should. Do not attempt to correct either of these problems since there is nothing they can do about it unless their rigger is shimmed down. If you do not have any shims or your coach does not want you to bother, the oarsman with the large thighs will get "stuck" at the finish and drag his blade on the water. For a description about shims, see Chapter Three, Safety and Personal Equipment. Short oarsmen rowing with a high rigger will have the opposite problem. They will have a hard time keeping their blade buried. Shimming the rigger up or using a seat pad will help or correct the problem.

Drills to work on blade height problems include **no blade height** and **gunwale high rowing** which give oarsmen an obvious height to aim for; the **1,2,3 rowing** and **1,2,3 set drills**; the **cut the cake drill** to work on the blade height on the first part of the recovery; the **eyes closed drill** so the oarsmen can feel what the correct blade height is; **inside arm only** for problems that occur at the rollup - skying, hitting the water, etc...; **outside arm only** for eliminating the feather and rollup of the blade as possible problems; the **finish sequence**; **pause drills** to see where the blade heights go off; and the **pick drill** for the same reason.

Drills that challenge oarsmen to focus on blade height problems include the **square blade drill** and **reduced feather drills** - great for those who hit the water on the recovery since they will have no choice but to keep their hands down; **circular rowing**; and the **Russian drill** which magnifies any problems. The **Russian drill** is an advanced drill and should only be done by those with more than a year of experience.

Practicing

BLADE DEPTH

Once an oar is properly buried at the catch, it is very difficult to change the depth of the blade in the middle of the stroke if the pitch is set properly. (see **Figures 10.8, 10.9, and 10.10**) A shallow blade is just as bad as a deep blade. Near the finish, oarsmen may end the stroke by easing up on the pressure and pulling the oar handle down into their laps. They may do this to finish quicker if they are unable to remove the blade from the water cleanly. This dump at the finish will create a wave as the blade clears the water. If the blade is feathered too early, a lip or wall of water is produced along with the wave. (see **Figure 10.9**) If the blade is feathered while still in the water, a **crab** results. A crab will pull the boat tremendously to one side and bring the boat to a near halt. In extreme cases, oarsmen have ben ejected from their boat after a crab.

Oarsmen must pull back their oar handles on a straight plane. This starts with a proper blade depth at the catch. The **catch placement drill** is good for demonstrating what the proper blade depth looks like. The oarsmen should watch at least a third of the strokes done during this drill. You can explain to them the proper depth of the blade and their adjustments are immediately visible. Blade depth also depends upon the angle of the blade as it enters the water. An over-rolled blade will washout, and an under-rolled blade will dig. See the section on Blade Rollup.

SLOPPY CATCHES

As seen in **Figure 10.4**, a perfect catch includes both foresplash and backsplash as the blade enters the water. The blade must be completely squared with no motion toward the bow or stern as it enters the water. Motion toward the stern will cause the blade to be rowed into the water; motion toward the bow will cause a large backsplash and a check upon the forward motion of the boat. Listed in Chapter Seven, Style Fundamentals, are the six simultaneous motions of the catch. The ability to match the blade speed to the water

Figure 10.8 A slight difference in blade depth affects timing and set.

Figure 10.9 Wash at the finish.

Figure 10.10 A dig at the catch.

65

Chapter Ten

Figure 10.11 Wash at the catch by the four-man (note the three-man bends his arms before using his back.)

Figure 10.12 Too much wash at the catch as the blade was jammed in.

Figure 10.13 The strokeman's hands are too close together.

speed is the most challenging of these motions. It is also very difficult to explain properly. Avoid repeating *You're rowing it in; Too much backsplash.* Instead, explain what the problem is and give suggestions - *Your blade is too slow, think of hooking the blade in; Try a "slam" catch for a few strokes.*

A good drill that works on the backsplash is the **catch sequence**. The **drag and glide drill** ensures that oarsmen quickly change direction on the slide and explosively initiate the drive. Drills that work on blade depth - the **inside arm only** and **outside arm only drills** - are also effective with sloppy catches. If an oarsman is not aggressive enough at the catch, go the other extreme and work with him on slamming the catch into the water. The oarsman should then average the two sensations/movements to find a perfect catch.

BODY AND HAND POSITIONS

Oarsmen must sit up as they row. Their backs do not have to be stiff boards, but they should have some firmness to them. Not sitting up in the proper position makes it more difficult to breathe properly, to pull in the oar handle fully at the finish, to maintain proper hand levels, and to reach fully into the catch. Most oarsmen will sit up in the proper position with a simple reminder from you, *All eight to sit up*. Oarsmen should also lean into their rigger slightly at the catch and finish. A lean too far makes the body tense and will throw off the set. Use the **wide grip drill** to force reluctant oarsmen to lean into the riggers.

For proper body positions see Chapter Seven, Style Fundamentals. The proper amount of lean into the finish is shown in **Figure 7.1**. A lean away from the rigger is shown in **Figure 10.15**. A lean too far into the rigger is shown in **Figure 10.16**. Drills to correct body position include the **inside and outside hand only drills**; **exaggerated layback**; **exaggerated slowness drill** to spot problems when they occur; and the **catch sequence**.

Improper positioning of the arms can also have an effect upon rowing. The outside arm

Practicing

and hand are primarily used for leverage, while the inside arm and hand are used for feathering and lateral pressure. Though the outside wrist is kept in a straight position on the recovery, the inside wrist is kept in a cocked downwards position. (see **Figure 10.14**) The inside wrist is straightened as it rolls up the blade.

Not every novice has good wrist strength. Drills for oarsmen who have too little control of their wrist are the **inside and outside arm only drills**. Do the **inside arm only drill** at full feather and a low strokerate with little pressure, but the **outside arm only drill** at square blades and a normal strokerate with up to 1/2 pressure. The **straight arm drill** eliminates the arms as as a cause for finish problems. The degree of arm usage can then be slowly increased to normal rowing to pinpoint where a problem occurs. The hands should be spaced approximately eight to twelve inches apart on the oar. (see **Figure 10.14**)

A common problem that is difficult to correct is a **lunge** at the catch. There are two types of lunges - into the stern and into the rigger. Oarsmen who do not fully compress will lunge into the stern with their upper body as they hit full slide. This will cause the stern of the boat to dip down into the water. Remind the oarsmen to swing fully forward by 1/4 slide. Use the **1,2,3 stationary drill**. Oarsmen who do not slowly lean into their rigger will lunge into it throwing off the set particularly those with a large upper body. Use the **exaggerated slowness drill** and the **inside arm only drill** although videotaping is usually the best way to correct both types of lunges.

SLIDE CONTROL

Another common error is to **rush** on the recovery toward the catch. (see **Figure 10.17**) This often results in timing problems at the catch. A coxswain must rely on more than a look at the catch timing to see if someone is rushing. An oarsman may be slow pushing his hands away from his body, but then speeds up his slide to be on time at the catch. A rarer mistake is to rush on the drive. (see **Figure**

Figure 10.14 The inside hand wrist is cocked up rather than down.

Figure 10.15 A lean away from the riggers at the finish.

Figure 10.16 Too much lean into the rigger.

Chapter Ten

Figure 10.17 A rush on the recovery by the bowman.

10.18) The oarsman who does this is most likely catching too early or rowing with too much pressure. The **pick drill** and **pause drills** will pinpoint the exact place that oarsmen pull ahead or fall behind. The **pair joining in drill** highlights which pair causes the rush. To make it obvious to oarsmen who swear that they are not rushing, row with **exaggerated slowness** or **eyes closed** to force oarsmen to follow their natural tendencies to rush. This makes it easier for oarsmen to believe you and perhaps work on solving their rush problems themselves, rather than you telling them.

PUDDLE SPACING

To measure the speed and effectiveness of your boat without a speed sensor, look at the bowman's puddle. If you are rowing at full pressure at a low strokerate in an eight, his puddle should be behind your stern by the time of the next catch. As the strokerate increases or the pressure decreases, the puddle will be closer to you, and at a high strokerate will be in front of you. Tell the oarsmen during pieces where the bowman's puddle is, *Three feet behind me. Let's work on clean finishes to send them back even further.* You will know that your boat is not rowing as well as yesterday because the bowman's puddle was three feet behind you while doing a full

Figure 10.18 Rush on the drive.

pressure ten at a strokerate of 32. Today, the puddle is beside you which means that on every stroke your boat is three feet slower than yesterday. Reasons for the distance changing range from more/less power to better/worse technique or set.

> When I would need to wait for another boat to catch up to me during practice, I would do the stationary finish drill and the catch placement drill to keep everyone alert.

> On my college varsity boat, I would often combine drills like square blades, eyes closed and the cut the cake drill to make things challenging.

Feel free to modify or combine drills to solve whatever problems occur. Your initiative should include the pressures, strokerates, and times within the workout for drills. By the end of the season, you should be able to combine several drills at once - perhaps **pause drills** at **square blades**, and perhaps with **eyes closed** and **feet untied** for the more advanced boats. There is never a time when drills are not "needed." Even if the boat's rollup timing is perfect, do rollup drills as a reminder. Practice makes perfect, though there is no perfect in rowing - only better.

Chapter Eleven
Landing

Your ability to land correctly is one of your most visible accomplishments as a coxswain. The large number of shells with a different colored bow section is not due to aesthetic reasons. (see **Figure 2.1**) It is due to coxswains who are only capable of ramming the boat into a dock, rather than landing it safely. Some teams will paint both the bow and stern sections in matching colors in an attempt to hide this fact. Watching a poor landing can be great fun for spectators, but can hardly be described as enjoyable to the oarsmen in the boat, never mind the coxswain. Ramming a dock can damage a boat so much that a new bow may be required. Bowballs can only prevent so much damage. When you land your boat, pay attention! Practice may seem over, but it's not. Practice is over when you leave the boathouse with your shell on the rack in one piece and all of the equipment is in its proper place.

Until you have mastered the basics of how to steer a shell, your coach may land your shell directly by giving the commands himself. After a few weeks, your landing skills will develop to the point where he only watches for any problems and then eventually ignores your landing. Since your coach may be extremely forgetful or busy dealing with the catastrophes that tend to arise during the first week, a novice coxswain must be prepared to land himself from the first day of practice.

Those of you who come from a nautical background will have an easier time landing. The reason for this comparison is that the course of a 55 foot long shell is changed by currents, wind, and momentum just as other large boats are. Turning and stopping a large boat, whether a 55 foot shell or a 30 foot powerboat, requires a sense of caution and wariness in addition to an understanding of winds and currents. Even landings without wind or current can prove difficult for a coxswain whose teammates are "asleep at the wheel." As you land,

Figure 11.1 A good landing with a proper 15° approach angle.

Chapter Eleven

Figure 11.2 Crowding the dock...

Figure 11.3 ...and the result as the boats collide.

all oarsmen must be listening to you. No one will lay the blame on an oarsman who did not respond to your command to *hold water* or *watch your blade*. Landings are your personal responsibility. There is no second prize - land correctly or prepare for the grief due you.

If there are boats in front of you on the dock, do not approach too close as you may drift into them. (see **Figures 11.2 and 11.3**) If you do have to wait, pass the gear the oarsmen have given to you to keep, so that you can save time on the dock. If a team does take a ridiculously large amount of time to get off the dock, vocal encouragement on your part usually helps to speed things along.

STANDARD LANDINGS WITH NO WIND OR CURRENT

As you approach the dock, row toward it at a 15° angle at low speed. (see **Figure 11.4**) Stop rowing about 200 meters (10 lengths) away from the dock, *Weigh enough*. Continue the approach with only stern four rowing, *Stern four only to row, ready, row*. This allows your bow pair to join in as necessary to assist your steering. Using bow four rowing with stern pair assisting your steering is not as helpful. Since you are not worried about set during landing, do not worry about cranking the rudder to one side if necessary. Aim to hit the middle of the dock with your bowball at a 15° angle of impact. As you approach to within 50 meters (2

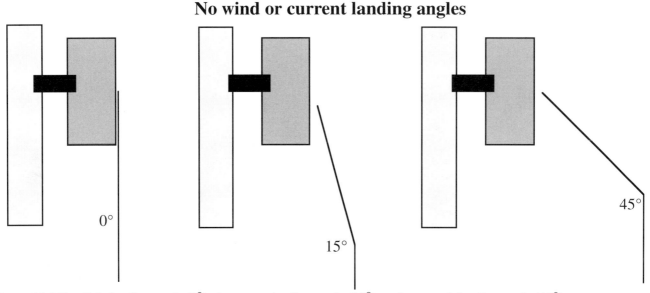

Figure 11.4 Too little landing angle (0°), the correct landing angle (15°), and too much landing angle (45°).

Landing

1/2 lengths) of the dock, switch to stern pair rowing only, *Five and six out on this one.*

A daydreaming oarsman may not only ruin a perfectly good landing, but also a very expensive blade by getting it caught under the dock. The momentum of the boat will either damage the rigger or snap the blade. As you approach the dock, warn the team to protect their blades by lifting them on top of the dock, *Heads up, watch your blades on port (starboard).* If necessary repeat the dock warning and point out people by name who are drifting out into space, *Watch your blade, Chris.* Tell your crew to lean away from the dock to prevent the riggers from absorbing any impact, *Lean to starboard (port).* When your bowball crosses the near edge of the dock, stop rowing, *Weigh enough.* The two-man's (bowman's) oar should be unable to row since it should now be on top of the dock.

As the shell continues to drift, the dragging of the blades touching the water on one side will cause the boat to turn about 15°. This is the reason for the initial 15° approach angle. Do not go over this angle. If you do, your bow will hit the dock since the dragging blades will not turn the boat enough. If you land at less than a 15° angle, the landing will be more difficult and you may swing your stern into the near corner of the dock as the blades drag.

If your approach angle is greater than 15°, but there is room to correct it, steer toward the beginning of the dock and then back toward it at the proper angle. (see **Figure 11.5**) If your approach angle is less than 15°, but there is room to correct it, steer away from the dock and then back toward it at the proper angle. Both landings will be more difficult, but at least there will be no permanent damage.

After the blades drag in the water, the boat should be slow enough to stop with a few grips of hands, *Fend off... pull it in.* Landings can usually be aborted. If your landing will not be successful and you cannot correct this, either row by the dock and make a U-turn or back the boat down. Then try again.

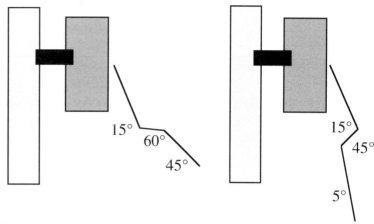

Figure 11.5 Corrected docking angles - too much initial approach angle and too little.

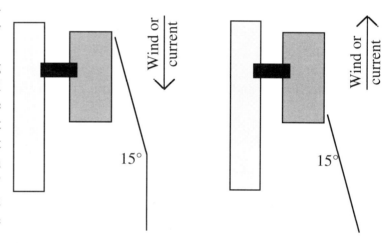

Figure 11.6 Proper landings with a head or tail wind/current.

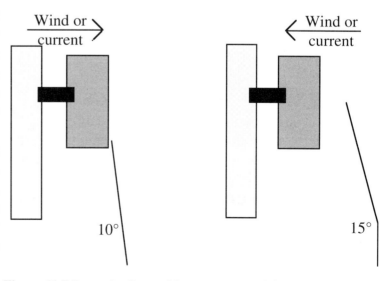

Figure 11.7 Proper landings with a cross current/wind.

Chapter Eleven

LANDINGS WITH CURRENT/WIND

Two forces, wind and current, will require you to adjust your landing speed and direction with an endless number of combinations. Think of four types of landings with only one force pushing against your boat. Landings with current/wind are not anymore difficult than landings without them. Only change your approach speed and/or angle. When a wind that has the same force, but opposite direction as a current meet, they cancel each other out though they leave behind a chop on the water's surface. Currents and wind from the same direction will create a very strong force from one direction for you to deal with. If the current and wind are from different directions, average the necessary changes in your speed/course that each requires you to make. A challenging landing that even experienced coxswains have trouble with is a strong current and/or wind pushing your boat away from the dock.

If you land into a direct head current/wind, row with firmer pressure and aim toward the end the dock. Use a 15° angle of approach. (see **Figure 11.6**)

If you land with a direct tail current/wind, row with less pressure and aim toward the beginning of the dock. Use a 15° angle of approach. (see **Figure 11.6**)

If you are land with a direct cross current/wind that is pushing you off the dock, row with normal pressure toward the beginning of the dock. The bow pair should untie and be prepared to jump out of the boat to pull you in. Use a 5° or 10° angle of approach. Remember that even the best coxswains may need help landing when strong winds and currents appear. (see **Figure 11.7**)

If you land with a direct cross current/wind that is pushing you onto the dock, row with normal pressure toward a point a few meters off the middle of the dock. The wind will then push you into it. Use a 15° angle of approach. (see **Figure 11.7**)

ESPECIALLY DIFFICULT LANDINGS

Docks which are perpendicular to the shore require a slow landing since your bow could hit shore if you overshoot. Land so slowly that you may be pushed off course. It is better to lose your point than your bow. On small docks, only a few oarsmen may be able to get in or out of the boat at a time. Land so that your bowman is at the end of the dock. As many oarsmen as possible should get out of the boat and remove their oars. They should then walk the boat down the dock so that everyone else can get out. The oarsmen on the dock should firmly hold the boat so that it does not flip. On very high docks, oarsmen must lean away from the dock to protect the riggers.

MORE EXPERIENCED LANDINGS

When you have enough experience, land by drifting into the dock with the blades in the air. Stop rowing much earlier to allow all of the forward momentum to wear out. Your team should anticipate your rudder turns to use lateral pressure to maintain the set. This landing looks professional and demonstrates that you are an experienced coxswain. Remember that if you fail at this type of landing, you will definitely look like an amateur. Do not attempt this type of landing until both you and your oarsmen have experience and only at docks with no strong winds or currents.

A coxswain will know that he or she has perfected landings if no one notices your landing. When you achieve this level, do not forget to remind your crew now and then of what a great landing you just accomplished.

Landing

THREE BAD APPROACHES AND THE RESULT

Figure 11.8 Too much approach angle and aim up the dock.

Figure 11.9 The result is that the bow hits the dock.

Figure 11.10 This coxswain has stopped parallel to the dock, but too far away.

Figure 11.11 Rather than back down and try again, the cox swings his bow towards the dock in the hope that someone can help him.

Figure 11.12 A coxswain goes too wide and at the wrong angle around another team on the dock to land

Figure 11.13 ...and has to be pulled into the dock.

Chapter Eleven

REMOVING THE BOAT FROM THE WATER

• **A coxswain should always stand near the stern of his boat prepared to protect the fin and rudder.** •

The method of removing the boat from the water is almost identical to placing it in the water at launching. With a novice crew, one side should hold the dock, while the other side exits the boat, and vice versa, *Starboard (port) to hold, port (starboard) up and out.* The team should remove their blades only after all oarsmen have exited the boat so that the boat does not flip while alongside the dock. The fact that your boat flipped once while on the dock will become a permanent part of boathouse lore.

> While on spring training in Tampa, my high school JV eight was in a rush to get to the cafeteria before it closed. After we had landed, the boat in front of us cleared the dock so my bowman and I hopped out of the boat to walk the boat up the dock to give the other teams behind us an opportunity to dock. After everyone on the starboard (water) side had removed their blades from their oarlocks before they got out of the boat to speed up the process, the bowman and I both watched in horror as our eight flipped over with our teammates in it. There were no injuries or damages except to our pride. Although technically the incident wasn't my fault since starboard side oarsmen caused it to happen, it was my fault since it was my boat and I'm fully responsible for what happens to it.

If an oarlock gate is stuck shut, use a rag or t-shirt to loosen it. The gates on the oarlocks should be shut immediately after the oars are removed, since they may be dragged across something and snap off if left open. Some teams like to exit the boat together and say something like the name of their team, the name of the next race, *Win*, etc... The blades should then be placed on the dock with the face of the blades up or put directly into the boathouse.

With a novice crew, ensure that everyone knows what part of the shell to grab on to and when to lift. Otherwise, get off the dock as quickly as possible! The time to reflect on a practice or discuss that night's plans is <u>after</u> the boat and all of the equipment is put away. If crews are waiting on the water for you to clear the dock, save retrieving the sneakers for later unless there is a pile of mud to walk through. Spending more than 45 seconds on the dock is a waste of time and will earn the wrath of other crews who are stuck waiting for you to move. It can really be done in less than 30 seconds if you try. This is even more true when the weather is cold, rainy, or windy and the incentive of getting into a warm boathouse causes everyone to move much quicker. Even if you are the last boat to land or you are the only boat at the boathouse, a quick exit from the water prepares for regattas where there may be only one dock used by several hundred crews.

Most manufacturers have preferred points for lifting the hull. The ribs are always a safe place to lift. Some manufacturers recommend the riggers and the foot stretchers, while others do not. Play it safe and check with your coach. On older, heavier wooden boats, extra people may be necessary to lift the boat out of the water.

There are various commands for lifting the hull. Novices usually take two steps. The first step is to lift the hull straight up to waist height - *To waists, ready, up.* A boat which is not lifted straight up will have its fin dragged across the edge of the dock, bending or snapping it. If the fin is in danger, help lift the boat while you push it away from the dock. Remind the strokeman to stand as close as possible to the fin. If there are cleats on the dock, remind the oarsmen standing next to them to be careful not to drag the hull across them.

Use a second command to lift the hull to the over the heads position - *Over the heads, ready, up.* It is difficult to carry the boat at this position. Unless necessary to avoid something like a high fence, lower the hull to shoulder height - *Shoulders, ready, down.* Warn anyone too close to your boat, *heads up*. If the dock is slippery or is a mess, warn the team of what to look out for and walk more slowly over it.

Landing

STORING YOUR BOAT

If you row in salty or heavily polluted water, rinse all the equipment with fresh water to prevent corrosion. Even in fresh water areas, an occasional rinsing helps maintain the boat, keeps it looking professional, and reduces friction from dirt on the hull. Newer hull materials are relatively impervious to salt, but older fiberglass and wooden hulls corrode quickly under these conditions. Wash any electronic equipment that remains inside the hull along with the slides and oarlocks. If you are in a hurry, wash the boat while the oarsmen hold it at waist height though it is easier to do if you put the boat on a washing rack or slings. Put the boat on the washing rack or slings so that the bars properly balance the weight of the hull - under two-man's and seven-man's seats. If you use slings, turn them so that the gunwales rest on the metal bars of the sling, not the fabric. Since this is an unstable position, a few oarsmen should hold the boat. While you wash the boat, the remaining oarsmen should clean up the area and put away the oars.

After washing the boat, lift and align the boat to whatever direction is best for easy entry into the boathouse. If the boat must be brought through a narrow doorway, one side of the boat should be at waist height and the other at shoulders to tilt it, *Starboard to stay at shoulders, port to waists, ready, down. Watch the riggers on the door.* The bottom riggers should not drag on the ground. When the boat is placed on the rack, align the rack bars with the ribs of the boat. This helps support the hull properly and evenly distributes the weight. Each bar should touch the hull, but not a rigger. A misaligned bar or a rigger resting on a bar can cause a hull to warp. <u>Never</u> step over the boat as you put it away. A small slip can result in a large hole.

If the boat is stored outside, tie the boat to the slings or rack so that it cannot be pushed over by the wind. If you have a cloth hull cover, use it. If the boat and oars are stored outside on blocks, put the oars underneath the hull to protect and hide them from any curious thieves. It is a lot easier to steal a blade than a boat. (see **Figure 11.14**) After the boat is properly stored, put away any remaining equipment left on the dock before having any meetings. This assures that all equipment makes it back to the correct storage area. Equipment left on a dock can disappear mysteriously. At over $300 per oar, forgetfulness can be expensive.

If you own any electronic equipment that needs to be recharged, plug it in after ensuring that the connection is solid. Tell your coach about any broken equipment in the boat or new obstructions on the course so that he will have time to fix them or warn the other coxswains. If you are one of the last to leave the boathouse, lock all of locks on the windows, doors, and bay doors, turn the heat on low to prevent pipes from freezing, turn the lights off if necessary, and activate any alarm system.

Never think that your practice is over when you finish your last piece of the day. Landing and putting the boat away properly must come first before you can really relax and go home. Then, practice is over.

Figure 11.14 A boat properly stored on blocks, protected by a cloth, and tied down to prevent wind from pushing it off.

Chapter Twelve

On Land Workouts

• **Always stretch and do some warmup exercises for more than 10 minutes prior to any workout.** •

Training on land is an integral part of rowing to supplement on-the-water workouts and to replace rowing when regulations, weather conditions, or the season requires it. Even if you always train in warm and calm conditions, land training is important to highlight specific physical motions. Workouts on land can never simulate all of the motions of rowing, though a large variety of workouts can come close. This variety is also important to keep things interesting.

Though your role as a coxswain does not require doing these activities to improve your physical skills, do not ignore or skip these workouts. Since these workouts are part of the team's development, they are also part of yours. How much you workout with the team is key to being appreciated. When you complete the same workouts as your team, though obviously not as quickly or with the same amount of weight, your team will have a much greater respect for you than a coxswain who stands around with a watch and calls out time.

If oarsmen go running together as a boat, buy a pair of running shoes and get moving. If ergometer training is used, get on the ergs and pull. There will be a few laughs by oarsmen as you first attempt this, so be prepared for some verbal abuse. Try to row on an ergometer for a few times with no one around to get used to it and give yourself an indication of your abilities. Remember that no one expects you to pull as hard, row as far, or run as fast as oarsmen. If you did, you should be rowing, not coxing. If an oarsman gives you a large amount of grief for not being in shape the same as he is, remind him of this fact.

RUNNING

The basic endurance workout is running. Long distance running improves overall aerobic capacity; short distance running improves speed. You may actually be faster than several of your oarsmen, particularly in short, speed work - you have a lot less weight to get moving quickly. There are also oarsmen who are awful runners, but extremely fast on the water. Do not make a direct comparison of someone's on-the-water and off-the-water talents. A few oarsmen may have poor knees and require knee braces to run. Knee braces prevent knees from coming out of alignment. If someone forgets his knee brace, do not make him go running! Have him do something else that day that does not have as much impact upon his legs such as erging or biking.

STADIUMS

• **Never run on wet surfaces!** •

A quicker workout than running on the road is running up flights of stairs, called stadiums. Stadiums are often thought to cause injuries so do them properly. Most trainers do not like stadiums because there is a greater chance that someone will hurt themselves than someone who is just running on the street. The basic safety tips for stadiums are to never run on wet surfaces and to never run down, only up. Running down the steps rather than walking increases the forward, downward momentum and extends the knees further. This can lead to injuries from hyperextended muscles or accidents from falls.

On Land Workouts

ERGOMETER TRAINING

Ergometers are found in almost every boathouse. You should familiarize yourself with each type of ergometer in your boathouse - how to use them, clean them, and do basic repairs and maintenance such as changing of the batteries. Ergometer workouts are very successful at simulating most of the drive motions. However, your role in ergometer training is reduced. Ergometer workouts focus on increasing the pressure on the oar handle in competition with everyone else.

A very common problem that appears during erg training is incorrect hand levels. You may find that the oarsmen's hand levels are all over the place. If you train on Concept II's, place a piece of white tape on the wire cage to give the oarsmen a target height to keep the chain parallel to. Since there is a lot less for you to correct, you may be relegated to time keeper, water boy, and scheduler.

ERGOMETER TESTING

• **All oarsmen must face the same ergometer test conditions.** •

Unlike racing which can be affected by numerous variables - the weather on race day, how well everyone else in the boat is rowing, what the coxswain says, or how he steers - ergometer testing, rowing for a set distance and comparing the times, is the closest method to see what an individual oarsman's true physical conditioning is. As in seat racing, your job is to ensure that everyone faces the same testing conditions that everyone else does when they test. If one oarsman had to test with the glare of the sun in his face while another oarsman did not, you are not doing your job. If an oarsman is extremely late to his test, and someone else is scheduled to take the test when he finally arrives, the late oarsman should wait to take his test, not the oarsman who was on time.

Oarsmen may have testing preferences such as how much they want you to say while they test, whether they want to test outside or not, etc... Coaches usually permit these variances. Preferences such as what the ergometer settings are, what vent settings are used, etc... are usually not. Use your judgement and if you have any questions, ask the coach <u>before</u> the test takes place.

If an oarsman wants you to talk during the ergometer test, use some of the same motivations found in real races. Oarsmen should tell you beforehand what their time goal is. This gives you an idea whether to say *You're doing really well, three seconds ahead of your goal,* or *You're three seconds off your pace, let's take a big twenty to catch up.* Use whatever motivates the oarsman except commenting upon someone else's ergometer results or their position relative to him. Examples of what <u>are not</u> acceptable to say: *You're three seconds behind Jack's time, let's take a big twenty to pull ahead of him,* or *You're three seconds off the top four starboard scores, let's take a big twenty to pull ourselves into first boat.* Examples of what <u>are</u> acceptable things to say: *You're three seconds off your last score, let's take a big twenty to pull ahead,* or *You're three seconds off the top four starboard scores, let's take a big twenty to pull into that group.* Notice the very slight, but important difference between the second unacceptable comment and the second acceptable one above.

If there is a major problem with an oarsman's technique, tell him what it is in a slightly different manner than which you normally would on the water, *You need to adjust the ratio. Don't waste your power on the slide.* Emphasize what a correction of the problem will do for the oarsman - a longer stroke, more efficient use of the muscles, etc.. Even a reminder to keep the heads up should be handled with care. Oarsmen do not want you correcting them for minor problems on an ergometer test. From their point of view during an ergometer test, every problem they have is minor so you must emphasize how correcting their form will benefit them and their overall test score, *If you take the time to compress fully at the catch, you will use all of your legs to get that time even lower.* Just as after a race, you should congratulate or console the oarsmen after they test. A few words go a long way such as *Good job, you beat your goal; Congratulations, you matched your goal; Oh well, there is another erg test next week;* or *Don't let it get to you, it's only a number.*

Chapter Twelve

WEIGHTS

Another workout used by teams to increase strength are two types of weight lifting - heavy lifting and weight circuits. Whenever lifting weights, oarsmen should use a weight belt for lower back protection. Supervise a weight lifting routine so that an oarsman in trouble has someone to help him. Weight bars should not be thrown around or lifted with a jerky motion. All lifts should be smooth to avoid muscle pulls.

The first type of weight lifting is heavy lifting which is common to many sports. The choice of what lifts to use is best handled by your coach or trainer. Heavy weight lifting increases the maximum strength of a muscle rather than its endurance. During this type of lift, the larger oarsmen will generally outlift the others. Safety concerns during this type of lifting center on someone who attempts to lift a weight too heavy for his abilities.

The other type of weight lifting is weight circuits. Weight circuits are done for approximately thirty minutes several times a week, often done as a group exercise. This type of weight lifting increases the endurance of specific muscles, rather than the maximum strength by repeated lifting of the same motion in a circuit. The more aerobic oarsmen will generally excel here. Safety concerns during this type of weight lifting center on someone who throws the weight around too quickly risking a muscle pull or sprain. Oarsmen should do the full motion of the individual type of lift not only for safety's sake, but also to be more effective.

> Although I attended team weight lifting sessions in college as a coxswain/timer, I did not lift any weights until my junior year. Although I couldn't lift anywhere near what the oarsmen were lifting, I could sense a bit more respect for me since I made the effort to lift at least something.

As with any workout done as a group, coxswains should attend weight lifting sessions. If only one coxswain is needed, but both are available, both coxswains should attend. One coxswain can call out the time, while the other lifts some weights. If both coxswains cannot handle a full weight circuit at even reduced weight, switch halfway through the workout. The more competitive coxswain might workout while the lazy coxswain takes time or watches. During weight circuits, the job of the non-lifting coxswain(s) is often limited to taking the time and to signal when to start and stop. There should be little need for correction unless it becomes a matter of safety or an oarsman reduces the distance the weight bar moves. Overextending muscles or extremely fast repetitions of a workout demand an immediate response from you to prevent injuries. Suggest to the oarsman that a more thorough motion be used to slow down, or increase the weight.

Just as it's your responsibility to bring basic supplies in a boat, it is often your job to bring water bottles and a radio to the weight room. You may also find yourself in charge of the radio. Be prepared for some verbal abuse because no one likes the same music as everyone else. The music that most people prefer when lifting is best described as noise at high volume.

TANKS

Workouts in tanks are usually the same as the on the water ones. Your job should be the same. Motivating the oarsmen will probably be more of a challenge, but you will have a better opportunity to view the oarsmen's body styles and make corrections. However, finishing is usually more difficult in tanks. Do not miss a tank workout because you think you are not needed.

On land workouts vary from team to team. Teams who are frozen in during a long winter will have little choice but to use a variety of workouts during the winter. Teams rowing in sunny climates may never have to use on land workouts to substitute for time spent on the water. Whatever the reason for on land workouts, participate as fully as possible. On land workouts are not days off for coxswains.

Chapter Thirteen

Before A Race

• **This chapter is geared to away races.** •

Home races are very easy for the home team to handle. Not only is there an advantage in knowing the course, but there is also a psychological advantage in being familiar with the general surroundings and having more friends and family to watch the race. For away races, showing up to race is sometimes half the battle. There will be away races where you are just happy to finish because it was such a hassle arriving and preparing for it. You as a coxswain can limit these distractions and frustrations so that you and the oarsmen can do their best. There are also important things to learn in the days before the race that you may never have been taught such as how to back into a starting platform.

THE DAYS BEFORE THE RACE

Your coach will modify your practices several weeks before race day by doing starts regularly to familiarize your boat with them. Your calls during these starts should sometimes reflect what team you will be racing next. Mentioning your opponent's name is a great motivator and reminds the crew that every practice stroke counts, *We've got to have a great settle next week against Florida. They love to move out early.* Do not use the opponent's name as a threat, *We're racing against Florida next week and if we row like this, we're going to lose.* Use the pre-race warmup several times as the warmup for a regular practice. If no one likes it now, they definitely won't on race day. Begin to practice backing into a starting dock and having *Bow take two's blade* and *Two take three's blade.*

In the last days prior to race day, the coach will begin to taper the workouts to build up a reserve of energy. Shorter workouts will make the oarsmen extremely energetic and easily distracted. You should reinforce the need to focus on the days ahead. Tension within the team may also rise as nervousness about the race develops. Last minute equipment problems will further increase the tension level. If something in the boat needs to be adjusted such as an inaccurate marking of the center line on the rudder cable or a rigging problem, correct it several days before so that everyone will be used to the change. If anything bothers the oarsmen like a squeaky wheel, fix this problem as well. Teammate conflicts should be dealt with as well. If you are travelling away for a race and you know that two members of the boat absolutely despise each other, arrange the rooming lineup so that they are not in the same room together. A sudden drop in the set several weeks ago during practice would have only been a problem to be worked on. In the days immediately before the race, the same problem may result in a feeling among oarsmen of "Who is letting the team down by not paying attention?" Stop any conversations like this, *Everyone is responsible for their own stroke, so don't worry about anyone else's but your own.* If a few oarsmen cannot get the message, be blunt about it, *Shut up. We're all trying to win and you're not helping anything by talking like this.*

Remind the oarsmen to eat and sleep properly in the days before the race. The most crucial night's sleep is not the night before the race, but two nights before. Their meals should be nutritious as well.

WHO COXES WHAT BOAT?

In a program with only a few coxswains that have very distinct skill and seniority levels, boat assignments for coxswains are easy to determine; the senior coxswain who is the best of the bunch gets the

Chapter Thirteen

best boat and so on. In programs with coxswains who are not equally spaced in experience or seniority, coaches must make tough decisions. What about a coxswain who has only two years of experience, but is clearly better than the coxswain with four years of experience. Should seniority overrule skill? Since skill at being a coxswain includes experience levels, can this be the case? What about two coxswains who started the same year and are virtually equal in talent? Do you split the race schedule or flip a coin? What about a coxswain who has tremendous technical abilities, but cannot call a race versus a coxswain with poor technical abilities who is great at calling a race? Do you have one coxswain handle the practices, and one handle the races?

No matter what your coach's choice is, be professional about your actions and behavior. Though you will be upset if you are replaced by another coxswain or elated if you have moved up, there is no need to go around yelling about it, particularly in front of the other coxswains. Always remember that you are part of a team, and that parts can be replaced.

PACKING UP FOR A RACE

Since you cannot race with only seven seats in an eight, packing up the boat for a race must be done with great care. Inevitably, packing up for the race is done after the last practice when everyone wants to go home, eat, and pack up their own gear. Do not rush the packing process. If you or your coach asks if something has been packed and the answer is only "Yeah, I think so," find out who packed that piece of equipment and where. Otherwise, expect it to be missing on race day. Before taking apart a boat, establish who is responsible for what. Assign pairs of oarsmen to specific jobs. Generally, there are four areas of responsibility:

1. The oars, seats, riggers, and bolts for sectionals (Parts should be numbered with a permanent marker)
2. The washing and cleaning of the hull and equipment
3. Spare parts and supplies - tape, wrenches, slings, etc...
4. Electronic equipment - Strokewatches, electronic megaphones, chargers, etc...

Stack the port riggers, starboard riggers, and seats into piles so they can be taped together with white athletic tape. If the oars are not traveling on a trailer or van, tape pairs of blades together with a piece of foam between them. If you remove the collars first, the collars should be tied together. As the equipment is taken off the boat, look for any broken parts that you may have not noticed earlier.

When the boat is tied onto a trailer or rack, the knots should be secure. Tape the ends of the straps onto something to prevent any slippage. White athletic tape is the best tape to use. Tape a red flag or cloth onto both ends of the boats so that no one runs into them on the highway. Oars should be positioned so that the blades are near the back of the trailer and the oar handles near the front. Tape the shoes to the footboards so that the soles of the shoes are not permanently bent by hanging upside down in the wind. Bring enough slings so that all of the boats can be put together at once. Your final checklist should look somewhat like this:

1. All boats, oars, riggers and spares are on the truck/trailer/van
2. The oars and hull are properly and tightly mounted on the truck/trailer/van with a red flag taped onto any ends that stick out
3. Enough slings and wrenches are packed to put your boats back together
4. Enough petroleum jelly is brought along to place between the ends of a sectional boat to create a waterproof seal and to lubricate the oarlocks
5. All riggers, bolts, washers, and nuts are accounted for - be extra sure of this
6. Batteries for the electronic equipment are fresh and/or charged with the chargers packed
7. Soap and rags to wash the boat are packed

SHOWING UP READY TO RACE

Depending upon the size of the regatta and its distance from your home, traveling to a regatta can be relatively easy or quite challenging. Some teams travel cross country with a sectional eight or a four on top of a van looking to race, while others travel a few hours on a chartered bus, or even fly. Staying sane and

Before A Race

comfortable on these trips can be a challenge. Since you are not pulling the oars on race day, do not expect a seat by yourself in a van with a nice window view. Though you may be the key to victory on race day, the top of the luggage pile or the floor of the van is what you will get if space is tight.

When your coach travels with you, he is in charge and makes the decisions. If he is driving the trailer and has left early, he will have designated someone else in the van(s) to take care of the details that arise. He might choose the captain, the lead coxswain, or both. If this responsibility has fallen to you, use common sense. Your first and only priority is to get the team and equipment to the regatta on time and in one piece. Road accidents with loss of life have occurred due to distractions caused by rowdy teammates. The team should eat nutritious meals, not going from one drive-thru to the next. If motel stops are planned along the way, the team should go for a light run together upon arrival to unwind and stay focused on the race ahead.

> Although I was rarely the target of oarsmen hijinks while traveling, I was often tied up with white tape while packing up the boat for an away race.

On long trips with nothing to do, expect a few oarsmen to be extremely hyperactive. As long as they do not bother and annoy anyone else except you, let them. If they decide to pester you for fun, put up with the abuse for a bit and then tell them to hit the road. If it gets out of hand, good luck. You might suggest a stop for food or gas even if its 3 p.m. and the gas tank is full.

ARRIVING AT THE RACE

If your team has several boats, the boat used first should be closest to the dock and its blades the most accessible. Seniority is not a factor in deciding which boat gets which space, rack, etc... If equipment such as oars, electronic equipment, or even boats needs to be shared by two groups of oarsmen, work out the details now - Will the second group meet the first group on the dock? On a dock closer to the starting line? Or will the first group have enough time to bring the boat back to the boathouse/ trailer? Oarsmen are too focused on racing to worry about these details. It is your responsibility to not only know what they are, but also to communicate them clearly to your crew and to other coxswains affected by your actions.

When you arrive at the regatta, get ready for the race first and then sightsee. You are in charge of ensuring that your boat is put together properly. If this is one of your first races, ask a more senior coxswain for help. Look to see that:

1. Each rigger is at the right seat and tightened with the proper pressure
2. The topnuts on each oarlock are slightly more than finger tight
3. The hull, track, and oarlocks are clean and did not pick up any dirt from the trip
4. The fin is attached tightly to the hull
5. The **bowclip** is securely attached next to the bowball
6. The seats are attached to the slides and face the proper direction
7. All electronic systems are working and the batteries for them are fully charged
8. All oars are accounted for and were not damaged during the trip
9. Your toolbag contains a full supply of tools and basic spare parts

After your boat is ready to race, walk around the areas for launching, landing, obtaining water, and weighing-in. On race day, you do not need to discover that there is no water at the boathouse to fill your water bottles or that the launching dock is different from the landing dock. It is easy to lose focus of the race at a large regatta with many distractions. Remind the team that they have trained for the race, not sight-seeing or buying t-shirts. This does not mean that you are a dictator trying to prevent your teammates from having fun. Just make sure that the oarsmen are more concerned about their race than the price of the official program.

A key part of a coxswain's ability to successfully navigate the course is to go over all of the course in a launch or row over it with the team. Rowing over a course is the better of the two choices, but at smaller races

Chapter Thirteen

you may be racing shortly after you arrive and time will be limited. In this case, riding in a launch over the entire sprint course is acceptable. If a time has not been announced when coxswains will be taken over the course, ask for it and firmly make your case that you want/need to do this. You may wind up driving a small launch by yourself, but the host team or committee should have a planned time for all coxswains to see the course. Even if you raced on the course last year, see it again. Landmarks, river conditions and traffic patterns can change. At larger races and regattas, a row over the entire course and warm-up area is better for you and the oarsmen. Unlike smaller races, there will be numerous crews to distract you as you determine where you are on the course. You will want to know where to call the moves. Not all courses have the 500 meter marks clearly identified. At a smaller race, a large oak tree may be the 1140 meter mark.

THE NIGHT BEFORE

Sleep and a well-balanced meal are vital to the next day's performance. Every athlete knows what he or she can and cannot eat. Let them decide. Pasta is the universal favorite. In races with no minimum coxswain weight, your meals beforehand will not be feasts. Your teammates will ensure that your plate has barely anything on it. Stick to a small meal to keep you alive and your weight down.

> I preferred to be very calm the day before racing, usually reading quietly so I could go nuts on race day.

Coxswains prepare mentally for races in various ways. Some like to be active the night before, playing video games or going out to a movie. Others are more calm the night before staying at home, in their dorm, or hotel quietly reading a book or watching television to save up their "activity energy" for the race.

Prior to an early lights out, your coach may have a team meeting to go over the next day's schedule and strategy. Since you are the one who will be calling the shots on the water, the team meeting is not the time to learn what the race plan is. Everyone should know several days or weeks ahead of time what the race plan is. This meeting is the time for the team to memorize when they must be in a particular place such as breakfast, van departure, the weigh-in time for lightweights, shove time, and race time. Hopefully, you already know when these required times are, since you will often have times of your own to follow. There may be a coxswains'/ coaches' meeting, coxswain weigh-in, and bow number checkout. This meeting the night before is not a time for last minute hesitancies or problems to be discussed. Know what the weather forecast is and talk to the crew about it. Remind them to dress appropriately and where to expect rough conditions on the course. Remind them to let you call the shots. Your job is to cox; theirs is to row.

RACE MORNING AND BREAKFAST

> At a key early morning collegiate race, my boat woke up late and failed to warmup thoroughly before the race. As a result we lost by several lengths and only felt warmed up after we had already lost. Two weeks later, we won by a length over the same boat after a proper warmup.

A slow wakeup combined with a sluggish warmup can ruin several months of preparing for the race. A boat that is not thoroughly warmed up will be slower off the starting line for at least the first ten or twenty strokes. It is rather embarrassing to realize later that you could have won the race if your boat had been more awake and faster off the line. The whole team must be fully awake and moving around at least two hours before the shove time. Meal arrangements should have been made beforehand. If your race is very early in the morning, no one will want to eat anything substantial. Coffee and donuts will probably do for most. Full breakfasts and lunches can precede races that occur later in the day. Pancakes and waffles are the universal favorite. Apple juice is the best juice to drink since it most resembles the natural acid balance in the stomach. The acids in orange juice will ruin an oarsman's stomach during a race. Since there will be plenty of lactic acid

Before A Race

in the muscles from rowing, milk isn't a good idea either.

Have something more than coffee and donuts if possible. Being nervous at the line will make your upset stomach even worse. An apple, banana, or even a real meal will help calm your stomach. Do not make breakfast a public affair for your teammates to watch you add extra weight. You have no need to be paranoid about your food, though all oarsmen are. If you are over the weight limit, use your best judgement to minimize any weight gained from a breakfast. Lightweights must know their weight beforehand to determine if they are close to the weight limit.

Tension within the boat can also cause a slow start of the line. Race morning is a very hectic and stressful time for all oarsmen, coxswains, and coaches. A coxswain can eliminate some of this stress by showing leadership and handling any problems that may arise such as delays, general confusion, and missing people without showing any discomfort. Part of being a leader is exercising leadership.

PRE-RACE MEETINGS

Most regattas have pre-race meetings for coaches, coxswains, and referees. Attend the appropriate meetings even if attendance is not mandatory. Though you may have raced in the same regatta for years, rules, traffic patterns, and locations of obstructions can change. Information mailed prior to the race may also have changed and/or be inaccurate regarding rules and times to launch, etc... Discovering for the first time that an official bow number is needed while about to shove off the dock only distracts the crew, limits warmup time, and earns you the wrath of the officials and possible penalties that you deserve for being an uninformed coxswain. A row over the course the day before should have answered your basic questions such as where the start is and what the buoy colors are.

Do not hesitate to ask <u>intelligent</u> questions at these pre-race meetings. These meetings are held partially for the benefit of the referees to spread the rules of the regatta and partially to answer questions asked by coaches and coxswains. Ask any questions that you might have except for those already answered in a race instruction booklet that you neglected to read the night before. Do your homework and do not ask dumb questions. After attending several of these meetings, you will see the same clueless coxswains ask what the starting commands are or what the traffic pattern is even though that information was already handed out.

Knowing what team is in what lane is your responsibility. If you are racing in a head race, write down and/or memorize the teams in front of you and behind you for at least five boats in each direction. This knowledge comes in handy when trying to pass a boat not only to spur your own crew on, but also to call out to them when you want to pass. When you launch, look for these and memorize what they look like and their blade colors. This knowledge will help to gauge your competition and to locate your proper starting position if someone's bow number falls off.

THE WEIGH-IN

Races for lightweights will have a weigh-in; a few will use the honor system. You or the coach should be in charge of organizing your boat's weigh-in. When there is a possibility that the entire boat average will be too high, the boat should watch what they eat. Hopefully, your coach has set individual weight targets for everyone on the boat so that everyone will be conscious of their own weight. If someone's weight is individually too high, he will need to run it off or be substituted for. If someone's weight causes the boat average to be too high, your coach must make the decision to make him lose it or make the whole team. If it is only a pound or two, the guilty oarsman should be responsible for losing the weight. If the weight that needs to be lost is too great for someone to do, the whole team may be forced to lose weight or a spare substituted for the overweight oarsman. While the team runs in sweats, no one should say anything to the guilty party. Team spirit is important for the race; save the arguing for later.

Races with a minimum weight for coxswains will also have weigh-ins. Know several days before hand if you will make the target and prepare any necessary sandbag(s). If your weight is only a few pounds too low,

Chapter Thirteen

plan on a big meal with lots of fluids to bring up your weight to the minimum. After the weigh-in, several trips to the bathroom can get rid of the fluids and the weight. Since there is no reason to weigh more than the minimum, plan to lose weight if you need to.

HOW TO LOSE WEIGHT

No one will disagree that losing weight slowly before race day is better than having to lose it all on race day. There is a limit to how much someone can lose quickly and remain effective for the race(s) on a given day. A coxswain has a higher limit than an oarsman. Most weight lost quickly is water weight. Oarsmen who must be in top physical form cannot handle more than several pounds of water loss before their body conditioning degrades. Water serves as the basis for hemoglobin which carries oxygen to the muscles. A coxswain may be able to lose the same amount since he doesn't need to be in top physical shape on race day, although this is a greater percentage of his initial weight. This sweat weight can be replaced by drinking the water back seconds after weighing in. Even so, heavy running before a race drains the energy reserves. You can see why it is better to lose weight slowly.

It's quite simple to reduce weight slowly - reduce daily calorie intake. The daily serving of ice cream may have to go. If the required weight loss is too high by cutting out a few bowls of ice cream, diet food may be the way to go. If you find yourself continually on a diet, realize that enough is enough. Lightweights must accept that they have to become heavyweights. Coxswains must accept that they cannot meet the maximum weight and let the coach and team know this. Most coaches and programs will allow some leeway. But when two coxswains are very close in ability, weight may be the deciding factor. If you do wind up on a lower boat because of your weight, remind yourself that everything has a limit. Some coxswains choose to become lightweights rather than endure the constant pressure to lose weight.

THE RACE OFFICIALS AND THE STARTING TIME

> At an away college race, the aligner was a big donor to the home program. With little rowing experience under his belt, it took over ten minutes for him to lineup each race at a floating start in strong current.

Though the choice of the referee should make no difference to the outcome of the race, try to find out who is the chief referee and aligner in a small race. This will not be an option for head races. You do not have to meet the referee, but just get a feel of who he is and what his skills are. Hopefully, he will be a USRA certified referee who knows what he is doing. If the referee at a small race is a parent filling in for someone, the race will not automatically be a disaster. Just be prepared for anything.

There will always be a specific start time to the race that should be adhered to. Larger races will obviously be stricter about the start time. The distraction of a false start for being late to the line is not needed. A false start may also cost you a race if you reach the limit of false starts allowed, typically two. Synchronize your watch to the official race time. This time is usually announced at both the coaches' and coxswains' meetings. Plan to be ready to launch and race five minutes early so that there is time to adjust for any unexpected developments.

PREPARING TO LAUNCH

If the shells have already been put together and you are staying in a hotel nearby, plan to arrive at the regatta at least ninety minutes before the race. This will allow time to look at the amount of traffic on the river, to know if the races are running behind schedule, what additions or scratches to your race there are, etc.. When you arrive at the regatta, immediately weigh in if you did not do so the day before, obtain your bow numbers, double check your lane assignments, and fill your water bottles. After these tasks are completed, double check the boat to ensure that everything is ready. Walk to the dock to learn the route to it. Watch several landings

Before A Race

and launchings to see if anyone else is having problems. Tape your bow number to the bowclip so that it does not fall off. If you and/or the bowman are required to wear bow numbers pinned to your backs, put these on your racing shirts now, not on your sweatshirts. If it is raining, keep the team dry as long as possible.

Your coach will hold a short meeting before launching, more of a pep talk than anything else. Close to launch time, the team should stretch and take a light jog to warmup. Your coach might take this time to privately tell you something such as *Good luck, you'll need it* or *You may be way ahead at the last 500 meters, so ease up to save energy for the final.* These comments should not be repeated to anyone except the strokeman.

ON THE WATER

Unlike the relative safety of your home course where you are used to the typical traffic, do not expect such peace and calm at a regatta. Every regatta has its share of problems and accidents caused by careless coxswains, oarsmen, and spectators. Pay attention to the whole regatta. It's almost like being an air traffic controller. Anticipate the moves of other crews both behind and in front of you. If you have to go around another crew, look around so you do not cut someone off. Sudden turns in a regatta generally lead to disaster, so make your intentions clear and then execute them quickly. Crossing a heavily traveled lane with only a pair or four rowing is asking to get hit by another boat or penalized by race officials. If it is time in the warmup for three and glide drills, hold off. Instead, cross heavily travelled areas with all eight with pressure.

Since your blind spot is now a larger detriment than before, lift yourself off the seat every few minutes to check what is in front of you. If in doubt, stop immediately. Though the traffic pattern on most American waterways is to stay to the right, some courses and regattas use the stay to the left rule. Coxswains who find themselves on a different traffic pattern than the one used on their home training area often forget this and are only reminded of their error after being involved in an accident. In Philadelphia, for example, stay to the left.

IF INVOLVED IN AN ACCIDENT

If an accident occurs, your first priority is to the safety of your team, not whose fault an accident was or how much it will cause the warmup to fall behind schedule. Ensure that no one needs medical help. Oarsmen are typically hurt in accidents by blades from other boats hitting them and by teammates' oar handles being rammed into their back. Bowmen are most at risk. Do not take an oarsman's statements for granted. If your teammate says that he is only "slightly" hurt and can row, but is not rowing well, do not trust his judgement. No one wants to stop the boat from racing and oarsmen will say anything to prevent a halt to a race. When an oarsman is bleeding or is blatantly having difficulty rowing, head for the nearest dock or even the shore, if you deem it necessary. While on the way to landing, get the attention of a referee for medical assistance.

If no one is hurt, identify the crew that hit you so that a protest can be filed later if you feel that it was their fault. If the accident may have been your fault or actually was, apologize for it now to soothe wounded emotions and quite possibly stop them from filing a protest later. The next concern after the condition of the oarsmen is the condition of the boat. A bent/broken rigger or oar will clearly prevent you from racing. Head towards your dock and repair or replace the damaged equipment. If there is not enough time, head toward the nearest dock in use by other teams. While rowing there, look for an official who might reschedule or delay the race. Larger regattas will often have a spare parts dock near the starting line to speed repairs of damaged equipment. If such a dock exists, head to this dock since the person in charge of this dock will also have a radio and he may ask the race officials to delay the start of the race to gieve you time to fix your boat.

The preparations for racing and the race day can seem overwhelming at times. Since problems with plans will often arise, maintain a sense of flexibility. Teammates who are flustered because of these problems will not be able to perform at their peak levels. Keep your sanity as well since you cannot perform effectively if you are frazzled or lack sleep. Your ability to handle problems in practice is a good indication of how you will handle problems on race day.

Chapter Fourteen
Sprint Racing

Sprint racing represents the majority of races. Distances for sprint races vary - 2000 meters for collegiate and Olympic level races, 1500 for high school races, and 1000 for masters. Although no two sprint races are the same, there are three general types when two boats compete next to each other:
1. A poorly matched race in which you have little chance of winning
2. A poorly matched race in which your opponent has little chance of winning
3. A well matched race in which both boats have a chance to win.

You can't do much in the first and second category to change the outcome, but in the third category of races, a well thought out and executed strategy can create the difference between winning and losing.

No matter how much an athlete trains to perfect his stroke or how great the strategy is, the human element will have a major influence upon the outcome. The possibility exists that one of the following could happen to prevent a victory when you are the better boat:
1. An oarsman catches a crab or somehow disrupts the flow of the boat
2. A wave or other unrelated occurrence disrupts the flow of the boat
3. An action that the coxswain causes disrupts the flow of the boat
4. A piece of equipment breaks
5. Your boat simply isn't the fastest boat on the water.

If any of the five possibilities listed above occur, the expected results can change a race from being considered a sure thing to a tough race. During these challenging races, a coxswain can have a large impact upon a team's performance. It's up to you to make the boat perform to its best on race day.

Figure 14.1 Properly positioned on a stakedock ready to race.

SPRINT RACING BASICS

The race is the ultimate test of the abilities of an oarsmen and coxswains. You <u>must</u> be prepared to handle anything. Even more important than during practice, your team should not look out of the boat, but rely upon you to tell them what is their position on the course. In addition to a planned strategy, selective use of additional tens and twenties can win a race. Your ability to project confidence about how well your boat is doing may not only motivate your boat, but also to demoralize and thus, slow down the other boat. Your voice must be clear, confident, and excited, but not so excited that you cannot be understood.

Before you worry about how to steer in a race, what strategy to follow, or what to say, remember that

Sprint Racing

there are four keys to racing:
1. The boat that breaks contact first (>1 1/2 lengths) and can maintain that distance for more than twenty strokes is usually the winner, even if that boat would normally be slower.
2. A coxswain must always be heard by his team - if they cannot hear what you say, you might as well be just a weight.
3. A coxswain does not have to talk every stroke of the race to be effective.
4. A poor coxswain can make the boat go slower; a good one can make a boat go faster.

Rely upon yourself on race day. Do not expect boat(s) racing in front of or next to you to be at the line on time. If your opponents are rowing away from the starting line a few minutes before the beginning of the race, do not follow them expecting extra warmup. Head to the starting line and if they do not show up on time, let the referee make the decision. Do not rely on someone else's course to maintain a straight line. Pick a target ahead of you and aim for it. Always follow the official rules, be where you should be, and be there on time.

SPRINT RACING STRATEGIES

The easiest racing strategy to understand is to row at a continuous pace and strokerate throughout the race. This strategy clearly does not appear in other sports and is not one typically used for sprint racing. Racing strategies consist of decisions where to make moves on the course. There should be a noticeable increase in power during the planned moves of the race. Though the strokerate may increase by two or three strokes a minute, the faster boat speed should not only be due to the increased strokerate, but also to increased power. Teams typically incorporate these moves at the 500 meter marks. Some teams in 2000 meter races prefer to move at the 500 meter, 800 meter, 1200 meter, and 1500 meter marks. The point of these moves is three-fold: to attempt to pull away from the competition, to "wake up" the team, and to provide oarsmen with a clear indication of how far they have raced/ to go. No race strategy is set in stone. If your opponent makes a move at 950 meters down and begins to move away, do not wait to take your planned move at the 1000 meter mark.

A typical race plan begins with a high (strokerate) twenty or thirty strokes. The strokerate should then **settle** to anywhere from 36/37 for experienced college varsity boats to 30/31 for novice high school boats. The oarsmen should anticipate the settle and accomplish it quickly. It should be the most practiced move during the days before the race. Since the body of the race is the longest portion, it is imperative that a crew shift the rate downwards instantaneously. Call at least one ten as you settle to get the boat used to the lower strokerate.

Once the boat settles, you may have some idea of the difficulty of the race ahead based upon your early position? Since this is not always clear, the boat should take a move near the 500 meter mark. A longer halfway move often occurs on a 2000 meter course. This move is usually twenty strokes in duration, possibly longer. Some teams will take a shorter move at the 800 meter mark and then respond to whatever the other team does. This usually results in a move at the 800 meter mark followed by another at the 1000 meter mark where the other teams try to pull away.

On 2000 meter courses, another move around the 1500 or 1600 meter mark signifies the final sprint of the race. On 1500 meter races, the move at the 1000 or 1200 meter mark signifies this final sprint. On 1000 meter courses, a move near the 750 signifies the final sprint. This move will likely increase the strokerate by two or three strokes per minute. The higher strokerate is usually maintained as the new base strokerate for the remaining 500 or so meters. For crews that have a tendency to fall apart at high strokerates or do not have much endurance, allow the strokerate to naturally fall off once this move is completed.

The final sprint of approximately 150 meters must be specific in length. Sometimes you will have no choice but to sprint earlier than you planned or think you should. There is usually no need to sprint early if the other team is still even with your boat. The only reason to sprint early if you are ahead is if your opponent had great sprinting abilities and they were only a seat or two down.

Chapter Fourteen

RACING AGAINST A VASTLY SUPERIOR BOAT

If you anticipate being in a race with no chance of winning, the only strategy is to get ahead early and hope for the best - the **fly and die** strategy. Instead of a hard 20-40 strokes at the beginning of the race, consider more if your boat can handle it, and only if. There is no point destroying any chance you have by forcing the starting sprint to a length that your boat becomes inefficient. If you can gain an early edge on the other boat, try to maintain that edge by giving constant encouragement without being artificial, *We're up by three seats, let's maintain the flow. Stay focused on the person in front of you, and don't worry about the other boat. They're racing their race and we're racing ours.* If the other boat takes a move, let your boat know what they're doing without sugar coating the facts. Remind your boat to stay focused and if the time is right, match the move.

If you do begin to fall behind, do everything possible to stay within contact, *We're down by four seats. Let's not let them get any more than that. We need to stay close so we can move back on them at our 1000 meter move.* Most opponents who never expected you to be a challenge will stop moving away from you after they are one or two lengths ahead. There are still opportunities for your boat to pull even. Unfortunately, these opportunities are generally due to the other team's mistakes. You may be two lengths behind, but a crab by your opponent is a severe equalizer. Don't let your boat fall apart and replace its hunger for racing with a desperation to finish the race. This sudden opportunity to gain the distance back would be lost. If your boat had still been rowing well, your opponent's crab might have been the break you needed to come back to win the race. As the phrase says, "It ain't over, till it's over!"

RACING AGAINST A VASTLY INFERIOR BOAT

One of the quickest ways to lose an easy race is to expect an easy race. Never cut back on training or pushing your team because everyone feels that the upcoming race will be a joke. It will be a joke when you lose because your boat was not warmed up enough, got flustered because your opponent used a successful fly and die strategy, or you only pulled ahead by a half length before your five man caught a crab. Never allow an "Oh, this will be an easy race" mentality to enter a crew's mind. Explain to them the fly and die strategy and have them look forward to drawing even with the other crew as soon as possible. Remind the crew to stay focused and not be flustered when your opponent goes off the line at a strokerate of fifty for forty strokes. If and when you do retake the lead from this crew, do not let the team relax and slow down. Do not allow a slowdown to occur until there is at least a two length lead. A great way to do this is to call a twenty after passing the other team's bowball, *Now that I've got their bowball, let's take a twenty to finish them off.* You and the strokeman should be the only ones in the boat to decide whether to delay or eliminate moves after you have obtained a comfortable lead.

NEAR THE STARTING LINE

As you approach the starting line, there will be less room to do longer warmup work. The line judges typically do not allow pressure work near the line due to safety concerns and the possibility that your voice might drown out the referee's. It would not be appreciated if you were doing practice starts near the line and accidentally started a race by repeating the starting commands. Avoid the immediate starting area - a distance of 200 meters or so should be sufficient.

Do not pass the starting line without making eye contact with an official so that the judges will know of your existence and arrival at the line. Stay within visual distance of the starting area to monitor the progress of the races. Listen to what the referees are saying. You might hear of a postponement, delay, or warning about weather or conditions. Starting judges will make every effort to inform you of any relevant information immediately, but cannot do so if you are headed into the next county.

For individual races, there is usually a fifteen minute lag between them, though at very large regattas there may be only a five or six minute gap. If there are fifteen or more minutes between races, you should use the

Sprint Racing

course to practice starts immediately before your race. A start followed by ten or twenty at a high strokerate, followed by ten strokes at the base strokerate will put the boat into a racing frame of mind. Within a few minutes of the start of the race prior to yours, proceed to the starting area. After the boats from the previous race clear the breakage zone, immediately enter the course to practice starts. It is not necessary to place your boat directly on the starting dock or stakeboat for the practice piece. Just start the piece within a few feet of the starting line so that your team will have an accurate visual clue to where the settle will occur. Do this practice start in your lane. <u>DO NOT</u> enter another team's lane. You may be disqualified and are asking for an accident. After rowing on the course, turn your boat around and <u>return to the starting area while in your lane at all times</u>, not in someone else's. There is no point in exiting the course and then entering once again near the starting line.

LINING UP AT A STATIONARY STAKEDOCK START

A common referee complaint is a coxswain who has no idea how to put the stern of his boat into the hands of a stakeboat/stakedock person. It is unfortunately a valid complaint. There are numerous coxswains who have never practiced backing into a dock and pointing their boat properly prior to race day. There is no reason for this and you should not be one of them. You will look like an idiot and your team will suffer as they may face penalties for your ignorance. Practice several times with the same oarsmen who will be in your boat on race day. It does take up practice time and oarsmen may not want to spend a few minutes on something that seems so tedious. Ignore their complaints and practice backing into your launching dock several times in both windy and calm conditions.

First, learn to back onto a dock accurately in calm conditions while maintaining your steering point. When you do back the boat down, leave the rudder straight and use the oarsmen to steer. The boat will be easier to control and unnecessary strain will be avoided on the rudder. Approach the dock from the downwind side and turn your boat into the wind. Obtain your steering point to the dock before backing down. Use the stern pair, four, or six to back down. Your bow pair or four can maintain your point either by joining in or checking one of their blades as you turn around to watch your stern. As you approach the dock, drop out pairs rowing until only the stern pair is backing it down lightly. Seconds before you would lightly hit the dock, have all eight hold water.

Your head may be sore as you turn back and forth to see if your forward point remains accurate and that you are headed for the correct spot on the dock. An experienced bow pair will come in handy here. As you gain more experience, you may be able to back down without having either point first, slowly turning and backing down into the correct position.

While the stakeboat person holds your stern, "locked on" as it is called, do not point your boat using the bowman or two-man. They will pull your boat off the starting line. Instead, have two-man take bow man's oar or three-man take two-man's oar to point the boat.

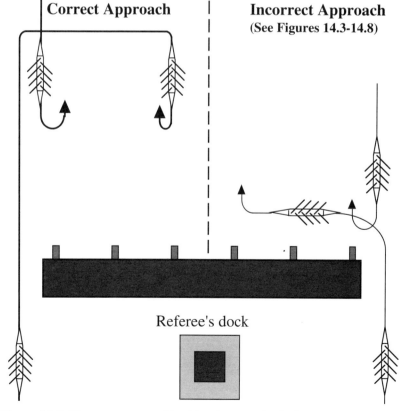

Figure 14.2 The proper way of backing into a stakedock start.

Chapter Fourteen

TWO EXAMPLES OF WHAT CAN GO WRONG

High School Championship

Figure 14.3 A coxswain is blown into the stakedock by the wind and now has no idea what to do.

Figure 14.4 Rather than realize her mistake and try again, she mistakenly attempts to salvage her docking.

Figure 14.5 While attempting to salvage her landing, she bumps into the other boat which did the same thing she did.

College Championship

Figure 14.6 This coxswain headed to the dock, but turned too late.

Figure 14.7 He has now trapped himself between the bridge and dock.

Figure 14.8 The dock person continues to fend off the bow as the wind forces the boat to swing onto the dock.

Sprint Racing

On a standard rigged port-stroked boat, turn the boat to port by having the three-man turn sideways and hold the two-man's oar while the two-man rows with the bowman's oar. The bowman's blade will now be almost parallel to the boat, rather than perpendicular as it usually is. (see **Figure 14.10**) Almost all of the force of the two-man rowing with the bowman's blade will push the bow to port, rather than forward. To turn the boat to starboard, have the three-man row with two-man's blade while the four-man holds both his and the three-man's blade. Since this procedure sounds complicated, practice this maneuver before race day. Do not use this method if pressed for time such as during a countdown start. It does take a few seconds and might not be finished by the time the countdown reaches "Row."

The other option is to have either the bowman or two-man point the boat by reaching out as far as they can with their inside hand only and then rowing lightly. This is easier to understand and cannot be messed up by novices, so your coach may prefer you to use this method if you cox novices.

TWO EXAMPLES OF WHAT CAN GO WRONG

Shown are two actual landings on a starting dock. Both landings ignored one basic rule of lining up: leave plenty of room between your hull and the dock while spinning the boat. In the first example a coxswain at a high school championship race incorrectly entered the starting area. (see **Figures 14.3, 14.4, and 14.5**) She should have continued rowing on the course for at least 100 meters and then moved onto the course. Instead, while rowing towards her lane alongside the dock, the crosswind that was not that strong pushed her against it. As she made this error, another coxswain duplicated it and wound up next to her in the same position. When they both attempted to swing their bow ninety degrees to the correct position, it only made things worse. They should have swallowed their pride, stopped trying to lock on, rowed down the course 100 meters or so, and then tried again.

In the second example, a coxswain at a collegiate championship race entered the course, turned, rowed towards the stakedock, but then turned so late that the wind pushed him into the dock. (see **Figures 14.6, 14.7, and 14.8**) While attempting the turn, he then became trapped between a bridge abutment.

Remember that both of these races were end of the season championship races. Both coxswains would likely have raced several times before this and should have been able to line up properly. Since it was a championship race, both coxswains' pride probably prevented them from realizing their mistake earlier and then trying again. Both coxswains continued to line up at great frustration and embarrassment for everyone in the boat in addition to annoying the referees. Their teammates are now distracted from the race and may not be as willing to trust the coxswain when he tells them that he can handle whatever comes up in the race. Compare these two poor examples to what these coxswains should have done as indicated in **Figure 14.2**.

LINING UP AT A STATIONARY STAKEBOAT START

When stakeboats are used instead of stakedocks, docking onto them is usually easier. Rather than having to turn your boat around, you can row from behind the stakeboats directly into the starting area. Pay attention to the numerous anchor lines which hold them in position. They may be only inches beneath the surface waiting to rip off a fin. Enter your lane from the upwind side so the wind will blow you into your lane. (see **Figure 14.9**) Except for these differences, a stakeboat start is very similar to a stakedock start as indicated in **Figure 14.2**.

LINING UP AT A FLOATING START

Floating starts require an aligner who has patience working with coxswains who may not know how to handle their boats. Work with the aligner and do not expect him to do everything. Use your judgement to assist him. At all times, maintain a straight point on the course. The aligner cannot accurately judge if you are pointed and will not appreciate you suddenly turning your boat by using the bowman, thus taking your boat out of alignment.

Chapter Fourteen

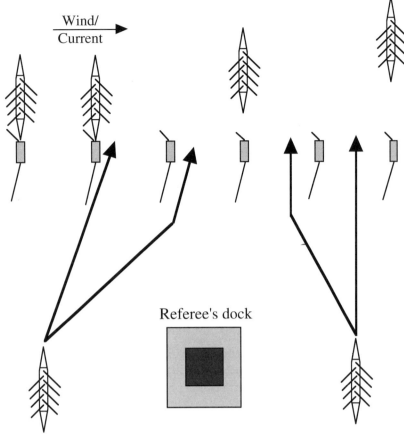

Figure 14.9 How to line up at a stakeboat start.

Think of a floating start as a very precise landing. As you come to within five lengths or less of the starting line, the aligner will ask you to reduce to stern pair only rowing. If there is a strong tail current, line up with the other boats at least 400 meters before the starting line. The aligner will let you drift or ask you to row along with the other boats in pairs or fours to move you closer to the starting line. If you fall behind the group of boats, firm up the pressure. If you pull ahead, lighten up. There is no need to race to the starting line. Within two lengths, he will ask you to come to a stop by drifting or by checking it down. He will then ask you to obtain your final point on the course if you have not already done so. From this point on, the floating start will continue like any other start. Most floating starts will use a countdown start that is not stopped if the crews drift. The actual alignment or distance from the finish may not be as accurate as that of a start made from a dock or platform. You do not need to complain about being down 1/2 seat at a floating start. Be happy if the boats are spaced this close.

The paragraphs above seem to imply that floating starts are easy and require little extra effort. This is only true when the weather and current conditions are calm. High wind and currents will ruin any start, especially floating starts. It will be a challenge for the coxswains, oarsmen, and aligners to keep their concentration and cool during the alignment. It is to everyone's advantage to begin the race as quickly as possible in bad conditions since oarsmen will get cold and tense while they wait. A successful lineup at a floating start is a mark of a good aligner <u>and</u> good coxswains.

CALLING A RACE

One of the most common questions that novice coxswains have is "What words do I use?" This question applies both to practices and even more so to races. As mentioned in Chapter Six, Communication Basics and Launching, there are no phrases or words that guarantee victory or that are useful for every boat. Each boat is motivated for different reasons and responds positively to different phrases. A race should be an extension of what you say in practice. If you have not figured out what motivates your boat in practice, it's too late now to think up those "killer" phrases. You should clearly mention the other boat when you talk, *We're three seats up on Florida.* Most coxswains will verbally attack their opponents during races. Some will only do so briefly, *Their three-man is weakening.* Other coxswains aim for a direct verbal attack, *Their three man is weakening. His puddle is getting smaller and he's falling behind. Let's take a ten to remind him of what full pressure really looks like.* Other coxswains may direct an even stronger verbal attack which cannot be printed here, *Their three-man is weakening. His puddle is getting smaller and he's falling behind. What a X. Let's show that Y and the rest of his Z-ing worthless boat what full pressure really looks like.*

What you say in a race may not have the desired outcome. Think of how you would respond to these attacks if this three-man was in your boat. Rather than ignore it which would only seem to verify it and demoralize your team, including the three-man, respond with a comeback/ attack, *Don't worry Tom [your three-man], they're clutching for straws. He's trying to make our great timing seem bad, because his is pathetic. With their sense of timing, it's amazing they showed up on time for their funeral today. Their bowman is so late, he's in a different time zone. Hey bowman [your opponent's], you should have learned how to set your watch before you tried to learn how to row. You failed at both.*

Figure 14.10 The two-man rows with bowman's blade to swing the boat into position.

If your three-man is <u>clearly</u> weakening, this response may be seen as insincere to the rest of your boat who may think you are just "sugar coating" reality. If his timing is that bad, acknowledge the problem in an indirect way and then respond with an attack of your own, *In two, up two with the hands, down two on the slide so the hands can come away from the bodies together. Picking those catches off with the man in front of you. Only 800 meters to go in this race so let's take a driving* [or more specifically, *catch timing* - if the problem is about to eliminate any chance of victory] *ten to shut this windbag up.*

Throughout a race on an away course, tell the crew what markers on the home course would have been passed if they were at home, *800 meters down. If we were home, we'd be passing under the railroad bridge now.* Let them know if there will be an area with a sudden change in the conditions such as a strong current from an opening to the bay, *We're coming up on a rough area about 100 meters in length. The current from the bay will come in from the port side.*

GENERAL COMMENTS ABOUT RACE STEERING

No coxswain can steer a perfect course since winds and currents will push you off course. Never steer off another coxswain's course. Steer your own course. Your only concern with his steering should be avoiding a collision if they drift into your lane. You need to steer the straightest course possible. A 2000 meter course should be just that, nothing more. Anticipate your turns of the rudder early to compensate for winds and currents. Recognize that steering is a trade-off to speed.

Referees are there to provide safety and act as an impartial observer and arbiter. Referees and race officials are <u>not</u> there to help coxswains steer unless one is clearly unable to do so and is endangering his own boat's safety or preventing another boat from having a fair race. The correct response to a referee's directions about your course should be <u>immediate and deliberate.</u> If the referee signals you to steer to port by calling your team's name and pointing the flag at you and then to port, lift/wave your arm to signal that you have heard the warning. Then move immediately to signify that you have seen or heard the referee's warning. Your strokeman should let you know immediately if he sees a referee signalling to you <u>and</u> what he is signalling.

The only time when you should not steer immediately to correct your course during a race is during a stationary start. Unless you are in danger of hitting another crew or being involved in another catastrophe, hold off on correcting steering problems during a start. Crews can have problems in the first few strokes that cause the boat to turn to a side - a washout, poor timing, etc... During the start and first few strokes, gaining immediate forward momentum is more important than a perfect course. A turned rudder will slow you down and

Chapter Fourteen

immediately put your crew behind more than an incorrect course. Once your boat gains its forward momentum after a few strokes, then correct your course. The only other time to ignore your steering is during the last few strokes of a close race, when your course will cause problems only after you cross the finish line.

On a perfectly controlled racing course, your job would be to steer a course from A to B as quickly as possible. However, race courses are placed on rivers, lakes, harbors, canals, and ponds. Sailboats, motorboats, canoes, scuba divers, and other assorted problems can wander onto the course. Combined with the appropriate action by coxswains, a good referee can handle problems with a few shouts from his megaphone to warn you and the people in the way. Nevertheless, your oarsmen must know what is happening. They do not need to hear *A 32 foot sailboat is headed directly at us with six people on deck who are pounding beers at every opportunity. We may have to stop.* All that is needed is *We're coming up on a sailboat that may be in our way. Let's keep focused as we go by them.* This informs your boat that there may be some noise coming up, you are aware of the situation, and you expect to move past it. Hopefully, your crew trusts your ability to handle various situations and will essentially ignore the problem and let you and the referee deal with it.

Since there is no guarantee that it is going to move out of the way, the possibilities range from steering around the obstruction to stopping the race. The decision initially and primarily rests with the referee. Do not assume that if you stop rowing, this is what the referee wanted and that he will order a re-row of the race. If you are concerned about the safety of your team, then do whatever you feel is necessary to eliminate or avoid the danger. Rowing is not just about winning races. Football players make lots of money doing risky plays which may or may not cause injuries. No one rows to get famous or become rich. Anyone who does this needs another sport fast. If you hit the obstruction in the hope that it will not cause much damage, you are likely to cause injuries to your teammates, damage equipment which is probably in short supply, and be unable to continue racing.

BUOYED RACE STEERING

Buoyed race steering provides coxswains a visual verification that their course is correct. Do not be satisfied with your steering if you never cross the buoy lines. You need to do more than that. The biggest error that coxswains make is to try to maintain a constant distance away from the buoy lines. Buoy lines are rarely perfectly straight. Always use a target in front of you to steer towards rather than keeping a set distance away from something floating in the water next to you. If you cannot see a target in the distance directly in the front of you, keep the strokeman's shoulders or head a steady distance off a target. Buoys can be moved by currents and wind, just as your boat is. Unlike head races, you are not allowed to cross a buoy line with your blades since this would interfere with the crew in the next lane.

NON-BUOYED RACE STEERING

Since no visual references exist to the side of coxswains on non-buoyed sprint courses, novice coxswains with a tendency to oversteer can seriously ruin a boat's chances of winning. If there is no reason to think that your course is wrong, leave the rudder alone. In a two boat race with only one target to steer for, the referee may tell the coxswains to steer to either side of the target. Hardly precise, but perhaps the only option. Plan on the blades being twenty feet apart at the finish line. Since you should have rowed over the race course before the race, you should have at least a general idea of the boundaries of the race course and the major meter.

In extreme situations, the finish line target may be a small rise in a hill or a clearing on the bend in the river. On foggy or rainy days these targets may be obscured until the final portion of the race. If this occurs, the referee should point you in the right direction. From the start of the race, assume that your course is correct unless you see a target that indicates this, the home team clearly heads in a noticeably different direction, or you receive directions from a referee.

Sprint Racing

THE START

Once you lock onto the starting dock or stop side by side at a floating start, the referee will wait until everyone else is ready. The aligner will then take over to align the crews. Try to keep the team relaxed. If the starting line is directly under a bridge or near another source of noise, every sound is amplified and highly distracting. Sounds from within the boat can be just as distracting. The start is no time to be stuck listening to a squeaky slide.

Once the crews are aligned, the aligner will raise his white flag. The referee will only begin the race when the white flag is raised. Any time the white flag is lowered, the referee will stop the starting commands until alignment is regained. During the period the aligner is in charge, <u>you and the bowman</u> should raise your hands while you adjust your point. In a bow-coxed boat, <u>you and the strokeman</u> should raise your hands. When your boat is fully ready and pointed, lower both hands. Only raise your hand when you are adjusting the steering, not when you are passing around the water bottles. Raising your hand signifies that your course needs to be adjusted, not that your three-man is thirsty or you need to reset your strokewatch. Referees are annoyed by coxswains who hold their hands in the air for no visible reason.

When all hands are down, the referee will individually poll the crews to see if they are ready and have their point. Fully raise and lower your hand to signify that you are ready. Starting commands vary from race to race. The varieties include *Et vous pret...partez, Get ready...ready all...row, Are you ready...row,* and *Sit ready... ready all... row, etc...*

At races where wind or current is strong, a countdown start will be used. The referee will count down from five to one and then use the usual commands. During a countdown start, the referee will not stop the countdown if your boat drifts off course or out of alignment. Fix your point yourself, but not the alignment unless he asks you to.

Whenever the final starting command is given, the referee will quickly drop his flag so the oarsmen can easily see it. Let the boat get moving by itself unless something is drastically wrong. This is no time to remind someone about a rollup problem unless it is blatantly causing problems. The first few strokes of the race is an easy place to fall behind if the rowing is poor. Blade depth should be perfect so that there are no washouts. Most coaches tell oarsmen to row at reduced pressure on the very first stroke - 80 or 90%. This reduces the chance that an oarsman will shorten his stroke by washing out so that he gets through the water quickly. Remind your team of this fact shortly before the start of the race, *Remember to row at 80% pressure on the first stroke so you don't wash out. It takes several strokes to get this thing to full speed.* Your initial commands should be mere indications of what the slide length is - *3/4, 1/2, 1/2, 3/4, full,* followed by counting out the number of the stroke. The start is not a time to make sudden steering adjustments.

Oarsmen will often be very tense during the start and initial 10, 20, 25, 30, or 40 high strokerate strokes. Several calm reminders to breathe and sit up should relax the crew and break up the monotony of your calling out the number of strokes. It seems natural to breathe, but nervous athletes tend to forget to breathe until they are out of air. This is the time of the race where a tense boat will be easily crushed. Do not expect the boat to be relaxed about racing. Screaming the words *relax* and *breathe* will only make the problem worse. Calmly, but firmly saying these same words will have a much better chance of being successful.

If you move ahead within the first ten strokes or are even, tell everyone including your competition immediately. In your voice the oarsmen should sense confidence and urgency to continue moving away. If you fall behind a seat or two, the oarsmen should sense concern, but not desperation. You should not lie to your boat. If you are ahead, you might say before settling, *We're up by a seat. Let's settle down five in two to keep moving away.* If you are behind a few seats, you might say before settling, *We're down by two seats. We need a nice relaxed settle to get that back. Let's settle down five in two. Ready, down five on this one.*

Chapter Fourteen

THE SETTLE

At the end of the high strokerate strokes, a firm and complete settle is needed to continue the race effectively. The settle is often the real beginning of the race as it initiates the longest part of it. A crew that rows at too high a strokerate will quickly burn out and fade into last place. Remind the crew to settle with their slide, not with their hands so that the slide ratio is maintained. When the time comes to settle, tell the crew what the strokerate is now, how many strokes to settle, and what the target rate is to aim for. Though anyone can figure out the math, do not give them the opportunity. You are the brains in the boat and hopefully you can handle basic subtraction. The commands for settling should be well known to the boat, having practiced it repeatedly. Typically, they might be *...5, ...6, at a 35, 7, ...8., .Ready, Settle down 5 on this one.*

Immediately after settling, take a move of ten or twenty strokes. Ten is usually enough. This allows the crew to row together at race pace while continuing the momentum of the start. Let your crew know how the ratio is, *We've got a good ratio, let's be sure to maintain it through the race,* what the rate is, *We're at a 36, right on target,* while encouraging them to relax and sit up, *Let's stay tall and relaxed.* Continue to let them know where the other boat is. If your opponent has not settled yet, tell your boat *They haven't settled yet, but let them burn themselves out. Maintain this rate and relax. We're racing our race plan, not their's.*

If the strokerate is too high or too low, do not allow anyone else but the strokeman to change it. The strokeman should only change the strokerate after checking with you. After all, the strokerate may be fine, but the ratio could be poor. Since there is no time to have a substantial discussion of the pros and cons, a quick gesture with your hand is probably all that is needed to change the rate - an Okay, pointing up, or pointing down sign. If you change the strokerate, make the command clear and decisive, *The rate's too low and we need to go up a bit to stay quick. In two [strokes], up two with the hands* or *The rate's too high. Let's not burn ourselves out. In two [strokes], down two on the slide.*

THE BODY

Your race plan is never set in stone and you are, along with some help from the strokeman, the judge of what changes are necessary. Changes may be required if something unexpected comes up or successful moves are made by other boats. Never let a boat break contact with you no matter what your race plan is. The only possible exception to this rule is if the other boat is clearly on a fly and die strategy by starting with a high fifty. If your opponent does take a successful move and may be moving away from you, try to interrupt their momentum by taking a ten or twenty of your own. Rather than deny the reality that the other boat is moving, or draw the proverbial line in the sand, *If we don't stop them now, we never will!,* use *Let's not let them get any momentum. Let's take a ten to match their move and beat it.* If your counter move is only successful in stopping their move, let it go. If the move gains back some of the distance lost, consider extending the move to either gain back all of the distance or to even pull ahead, *We really moved on that piece. Let's extend this move by X strokes to pull ahead even further.*

If your counter move is not successful, do not continue to remind the oarsmen about that fact. Merely let them know what the distance between the boats is and your position on the course. Make any corrections now in the ratio, rate, or timing. Being behind by a few seats is not a disaster, but being more than one length can effectively prevent a comeback.

Coxswains generally find the middle part of the race the most difficult to call. The start of the race is predefined by the race plan. The finish seems to happen too quickly. Whatever you say cannot be planned although you should have some idea before the race of what you would like to say. Other tens can be added to the race plan, but only a few. It is useless for you to continually count from 1 to 10. It is also useless for you to critique anyone's stroke unless it is blatantly hurting the boat's chances. If your boat has a particular problem that occurs often, remind the boat early what is needed to correct it. Taking a ten early in the race to remind everyone to sit up, lengthen out, or feather cleanly is a great way to emphasize correct rowing while

Sprint Racing

encouraging the boat to move faster. A great way to mention problems is to mention a frequent one for each oarsman in lineup order, *John* [bowman] *making sure you back that blade in, Tim* [two-man] *watch that sky, Fred* [three-man] *quick hands away, etc...* These problems should be the ones that these oarsmen have had before and are able to correct. By reminding them about them, they will hopefully remember that the way to win a race is through power combined with proper technique. Your goal is to set up a rhythm to the boat where everything just seems to float along.

The conditions of the course are another area to cover, *With this rough weather, get those blades in quickly so we don't get hung up at the catch,* or *We've got great weather so there's no reason we can't get those blades in quicker than them.* Another method of motivating the boat is to call a silent ten, *Let's take a silent ten on this one listening to the sounds of the boat.* This should not be done if the other coxswain is screaming so loud that your boat can hear him constantly criticize your boat. The option that is most often forgotten is to stay silent for part of the race. You do not need to talk every stroke.

THE FINISH

• **Do not call a sprint until you are sure that your boat can handle the distance left.** •

The last part of the race is the sprint to the finish line. It usually begins at 400 to 500 meters to go, but can come later than this. There is usually no need to sprint early if the other team is still even with your boat although sometimes you will have no choice. If the other boat(s) are relatively close or your boat is ahead, avoid the temptation to sprint early. Not only can this drain the team physically, it can upset the flow of the boat if the oarsmen subconsciously resist. The only reason to sprint early if you are ahead would be if your opponent had great sprinting abilities and they were only a seat or two down.

Teams usually increase the strokerate even higher during the final twenty or thirty strokes of the race. During these strokes the strokerate will climb to the maximum possible. This strokerate will be at least 7 to 8 strokes higher than the strokerate in the body of the race and up to 12. Form and style are almost irrelevant now; only crossing the finish line first is important. To speed up the boat during the final 20 or 30 strokes, rowing at legs and arms only without fully swinging the back will move the boat even faster. This final sprint of approximately 150 meters must be specific in length - X strokes, not X + 1 strokes. The oarsmen will plan to run out of energy in X strokes. Since there is nothing more frustrating than a race lost in the last few strokes because the boat ran out of energy too early, you must accurately decide when to call for the final sprint. Running out of energy is actually the goal of racing, but only after the boat crosses the line. Before your race, watch other races to see where the last X strokes begin. Know from practice how far X strokes will take you. Know where the finish line is. Don't forget that some finish lines are at an angle to the course. You may be looking out of the boat at the coxswain next to you, but actually be a seat down.

Racing takes up less than two hours of time for an athlete each year. Practicing for these races takes up a lot more. As mentioned in Chapter Ten, Practicing, remind your crew of the connection of practicing to racing. It is too late to correct a problem within the boat if you only worked on it two hours, two days, or even two weeks before the start of a race. When you cross the finish line in first or last place, your decisions over the past season will suddenly become clearer to whether a drill should have been used more often or the team was not in shape.

Chapter Fifteen

Head Racing

Head races cover a much longer distance than sprint races, so there is an increased focus upon aerobic conditioning. There is a greater need in head races for coxswains who know how to steer accurately and are aggressive with other crews. Even steering only 20 feet off the buoys around a turn can add an incredible amount of time to the result and will allow other crews to pass you on the inside of turns.

HEAD RACING BASICS

The typical distance for head races is around 3 miles. Since there are very few places where a straight three mile course is available, head races often incorporate several turns in them that can test a novice coxswain's steering abilities. Almost all head races station referees on shore to observe the race, rather than on launches following the crews. Since there are no set lanes that coxswains can steer out of, most problems in head races involve coxswains who steer through illegal areas, miss a buoy, or fail to give way to an overtaking boat. Know before the race if there are any expected problems from outside sources. In large harbors, there may be large barges passing through at a set time. There may be a stoppage of the regatta during certain times so that sailboats and motorboats can use the river or harbor.

Logistically, head races can be even more of a mess than sprint races. Figure out early on how to get your boat from your trailer to the launching dock while avoiding other teams rigging their boats and any muddy areas that often appear by the end of the day. Unless there will be someone on shore near the finish to throw you water bottles, bring more water than you would for after a sprint race. Rowing up to three miles to the landing dock after finishing the race without water is an unnecessary safety risk. On cold or wet days, bring gear to keep the oarsmen warm after the race. The extra weight isn't that important. If you think it is, have someone throw you the gear from shore or a bridge after the race is over. Since launching boats have priority over landing boats, there may be a long wait as you attempt to land.

Your starting position can have an effect on the outcome. It is better to be behind your desired opponents. Starting in first place gives you no one to catch up to, but starting last gives you too many slow boats to row through along with everyone else's wash. However, there is usually no way to change your assigned position.

Head races are started with a rowing start with each boat positioned approximately ten seconds apart. Unlike sprint races, your opponents are not directly beside you in head races to provide a visual indication of how well your boat is doing. You can rely on the boats in front of and behind you for only an idea of how fast you are moving. If you start last in a forty boat race and pass nine boats by the end, you may only be passing the nine slowest boats. The boat starting third may never pass anyone, but wins the race. If you start in the fifth position and are passed by only one boat, you will not finish ahead of that boat in the final standings, but you may finish second. Since many teams travel to head races, you may get an idea of how well you are doing compared to other boats you recently raced. Use this as only a rough idea and only as a positive indicator, *We're catching up fast on Florida and we lost to them by only seconds two weeks ago.* After all, they might be having a bad day or made major changes in the lineup between races.

Oarsmen in a head race must isolate themselves somewhat from what is going on around them such as more noise from the spectators and other crews. Provide lots of information about what is happening, including

Head Racing

distance from other boats, time rowed/ to go, what turns are coming up, and how other boats seem to be doing. Oarsmen should be concerned if a boat moves closer to them from behind and psyched if they are moving closer to a boat in front of them.

The best mind set for a crew to have is to plan on moving ahead from boat to boat as if climbing a ladder one step at a time. It is extremely doubtful that in a forty boat head race you could start last and then pass every crew so you could cross the finish line first. A reasonable goal would be to pass two to five boats that start in front of you. Since these boats may be very slow or very fast compared to your boat, your teammates must be flexible as to accepting what actually happens.

HEAD RACE STRATEGIES

All boats should be at race pace several strokes <u>before</u> the starting line to cross the start at race pace. Most teams take a high twenty or longer to get started. The settle strokerate will range from a 27 to a 35 for an eight. Race strategies can occur even before the race begins. If the boat in <u>front</u> of you seems to be <u>slower</u> than yours, you may want to <u>increase</u> the distance between your boats at the start to give your boat more of an incentive to catch up. If the boat <u>behind</u> you seems to be <u>faster</u> than yours, you may want to <u>increase</u> the distance between your boats to hold them off longer. You will only be able to decrease or increase this starting gap a few seconds before you are notified by starting line officials who try to keep boats equally spaced.

Unlike moves at various distances in sprint races, moves in head pieces are more effective at specific visual points - a twenty after the blue bridge, a ten just past the marina entrance, a silent thirty after the red channel marker, etc... These moves should be related to a particular problem in the boat such as rush, blade timing, sitting up, etc... In longer head pieces, style errors have more of an impact upon the boat speed than in shorter races. Use the moves as a way to correct/ remind the boat of something in addition to providing a burst of power, *Let's take a catch twenty as we clear the bridge. Get those catches in quickly and sharply.* A final sprint of at least twenty strokes should be part of the race plan. Even if you had a poor race, sprinting at the end will reduce several seconds off your time.

CALLING A HEAD RACE

What you say in a head race can have more importance than what you say in a sprint race. In a sprint race, you could stay silent almost the entire race about your position compared to the other boats since the oarsmen would have some idea of where they are on the course without even looking around that much. In a head race, your opponents may be far in front or behind you resulting in a tougher motivational challenge. As in a sprint race, the toughest part to call is the middle since the beginning and end is predefined by the appropriate moves.

Perhaps the biggest difference in calling a head race is a larger emphasis on style since poor rowing style will have a larger impact upon the outcome. In a sprint race a very slight lip of water from an oarsman's blade at the finish may not be that important to worry about, but in a head race, correcting it may knock off a few seconds from your finish time. As in an ergometer test, tell the oarsman what the problem is, how to correct it, and why it is important, *Jerry, watch your clean finishes. You've got a slight lip there. Try a little more downward motion with your hands before feathering it. We need all the clean run we can get to move down this course as fast as possible.* You will also have more time to work on large problems. In a sprint race you may only be able to quickly mention this problem; in a head race you can return to deal with the problem if it does not go away, *That's better Jerry, but a little more downward motion.* Remember that this isn't practice so don't spend the whole race working on his finish. Just point out the key problems and how to fix them.

Another area to expand upon is how the other crews are doing. Beyond mentioning the distance from other crews, expand upon this to include how they are doing, what strokerate they are at (either the exact one if you have a strokewatch or higher/lower than yours if you don't), specific problems in those boats and anything else that might be motivating, *Florida's three lengths up on us at a 31 [at a slightly lower/higher*

Chapter Fifteen

strokerate if you don't have a strokewatch.] Their timing is pathetic on port side. Their four man is so late, he must be asleep. I heard that they flew to this race while we toughed it out in vans. Let's take a twenty to close the distance between us. Port side keep your awesome timing to show these guys what the words "in time" really mean. Starboard side to sit up and demonstrate how you didn't need a cushy plane ride to get here. On this one.

Unlike sprint races, oarsmen have an increased amount of time to think about things that don't really matter - what everyone on shore looks like, is this the best race plan, why are we not catching up to anyone, etc... Be positive with your comments and remind the crew to focus on themselves and the race plan. Do not second guess anything. If you had a lousy start, don't dwell on it by saying *We had a poor start so let's make sure we get those legs down to make up all the time lost.* If you had a lousy start, but have substantially improved since then, you may, in a few cases, incorporate this into what you say, particularly near the end of the race, *We didn't have a great start, so let's really get our legs down this last twenty of the race.* This is a judgement call for you to make. As in practice, your silence is useful occasionally in head races when things are going well. Some coxswains may talk only half of the strokes in a head race, compared to 2/3 or 3/4 of a sprint race.

HEAD RACE STEERING

Unlike sprint races, head races include the use of steering strategy to take advantage of bends in the course, tidal changes, and mishaps that occur to other crews. Row over the whole course before racing on it. Any coxswain who thinks that a map will provide the best basis for judgement on a head race course is asking for trouble. A thirty or sixty second penalty for using the wrong arch of a bridge hardly does wonders for your finish time. Instead of competing for first place, you will be hoping to avoid last. Do not cut buoys! There are penalties involved, usually ten seconds for a buoy. Just as sprint races, head races are won and lost by tenths of a second. A penalty of ten seconds or more will deservedly earn the wrath of your coach, never mind the oarsmen who trained for months only to lose out on first place or something close to it because of your course.

Most head race courses are not totally lined with buoys. Buoys are used only to mark curves or distance. You are responsible for knowing where to steer when there are no buoys. Memorize what the colors or shapes the buoys signify. On some courses, colors differentiate between hazard and curve buoys. If you do not know the difference, you might follow a line of red buoys only to discover that it signifies a rock, rather than a turn. Use your best judgement on how far to stay offshore if no buoys mark the shoreline. If the course is relatively free of obstructions, you can be closer to the shore than a course with fallen trees and shallow areas. This would give you a range of 10 to 40 feet offshore depending upon the course. On courses with seawalls, inches off the wall may be an acceptable distance. If you have absolutely no idea what the proper distance is, do what everyone else is doing. It may seem to be crazy following someone who doesn't know where he is going, but if they don't hit anything, you probably won't. Not the best option, but sometimes it is the only one.

Good coxswains keep turn marker buoys under the inside riggers on a bend to reduce the distance rowed if permitted by the regatta. This is only desirable when the buoys are small, not directly over an obstruction, and follow a smooth path. Buoys that are not positioned correctly will require you to steer around them and negate any gains from hugging the buoys. When you cross over buoy lines, alert your crew so that they will anticipate a few blades hitting buoys, *Crossing over buoys on port side in two strokes.* On courses where the return traffic rows inside the buoy line, pay attention to boats inside the buoy line who may be too close and warn away if necessary.

PASSING BOATS/ BEING PASSED

The overtaking boat always has the right of way. There are requirements for both boats that must be followed. The passing boat <u>must</u> make its intentions clear that it <u>wants</u> to pass and on <u>what side</u> it will overtake, although charging up from behind usually signifies the desire to pass. If necessary, the faster boat should yell

Head Racing

forward that they will be overtaking and request that the slower boat move out of the way, *Heads up, shell passing on your starboard side.* The slower boat should move out of the way before a danger for collision occurs, approximately a one length distance. The slower boat must also yield the best lane to the faster boat, <u>if requested</u>. On a bend in a river, the overtaking boat will want to hug the buoy line, forcing the slower boat away from it. Coxswains being overtaken on a bend will often wait to the last second to move out of the way, in the hope that their boat will find a burst of power to hold the faster team off until the curve is completed. This does not always happen and as a result, minor collisions are common here. Referees are usually stationed nearby to watch for these incidents and assign penalties to a boat that fails to give way.

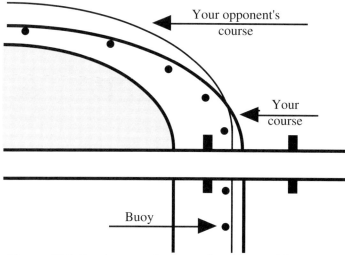

Figure 15.1 Passing on a sharp turn from the outside.

If you are the slower boat, move out of the way when you should. It might save a few seconds to stay where you are, but a 30 or 60 second penalty for failure to yield will negate this gain and then some. If you are passed on a long straightaway, there is no need to row behind them. The wash left by that crew will disrupt your set and slow you down. On curves, fall in behind the faster crew immediately since the benefits of a shorter course outweigh the disruption of rowing in their wash.

On long straightaways followed by a large turn, a great way to gain some room for experienced teams is to row outside everyone else to avoid all the wash of the other teams and having to steer your way through everyone. As you approach the turn, cut into the inside. If you did not pass everyone and there is a crew that has less than a length lead already on the inside just before the bend, do not plan to row on the outside of the bend. Since they obviously cannot move over because they are pinned between the buoy line and your boat, you will need a little steering maneuver to put your boat on the inside. Tell your crew to pay attention because you need to get the inside of the bend. Then do the following (**see Figure 15.1**):

1. Force the slower crew to hug the buoy line by placing your bowdeck next to their sterndeck- this will force most crews to go slightly wide on the turn
2. Reduce the pressure quickly to let the slower crew's stern pull in front of your bow as you enter the turn, *In two strokes cut to half pressure*
3. Firm up the pressure quickly on one side to swing your bow into hugging the buoy line as the other boat goes wide, *Starboard (port) side to full pressure to give us the inside*
4. Take a massive full pressure twenty to force the other crew to yield, *All eight, let's take a massive twenty to blow past them*
5. Scream about what you just did to further demoralize your opponent and psych out your teammates

The result of this move is that you have passed several crews on the straightaway without rowing in any wash, you got the inside position on the turn, you forced at least one crew to row quite a bit longer, and your team is really pumped up for the rest of the race.

Most oarsmen and coxswains enjoy head races more than sprint races. There is more time to demonstrate a crew's technical and physical ability, a greater impact upon the race from a coxswain in terms of steering and motivation, and a low-key atmosphere that is a part of head races. However, poor crews and poor coxswains may despise head racing because of the longer time to demonstrate their weaknesses. What you think of head races may depend upon the errors you make in them.

Chapter Sixteen

After A Race

After a race, there can only be two emotions - happiness at winning or disappointment at losing. You will also have one of these emotions, but you must be the first one in the boat to get rid of them. You must begin to look forward to the next race even before you land. A physical and mental rebound from a race will occur no matter what the outcome of the race. This rebound includes the resumption of a normal training schedule without tapering and shorter workouts. Losing should not be unexpected. You are not that good. No team is so great that they do not lose sometime. Losing can be a meaningful experience since it focuses the team on what it will take to win the next time. There are plenty of examples of a crew being solidly trounced one week only to cruise to victory the following week against the same crew with the same lineups.

POST RACE ETIQUETTE

Immediately after crossing the finish line, see if anyone in your boat needs help. An oarsman may be overcome by heat, dehydration, a diabetic reaction, or an asthma attack. If someone does need help, signal the referees immediately and head to shore. If no one needs help, do not make idiots of yourselves. Standing up in the boat and wildly cheering falls into this category. If you won, celebrate without insulting the other team. If you lost, decide why this happened on shore with your coach, not by having a debate on the water.

If you feel a protest should be filed over the actions of your opponent, make the protest to the on-the-water officials, not to the other team or wait till later. Raise your hand in the air and signal for a referee. After listening to your complaint, the referee will raise the red flag to signify the protest, rather than the white flag. Tell your coach about your protest immediately after landing so he can decide whether to pursue it. The initial decision to file a protest initially rests with you on the water, but the final decision rests with the coach.

Legitimate protests include your boat being hindered by another crew steering into your lane hitting your blades, an event which made the race unfair such as a massive wave which hit only your boat, etc... Protests which are not valid include boats that cut slightly in front of you while your boat was ten lengths back, a large wave that hit every crew, a referee's launch that waked you to keep up with the other boats, etc... Protests which are difficult calls to decide are a crew that briefly rowed in front of you in a sprint race when they were four lengths ahead. Even though you think it really hurt your boat's performance, remember that their course was longer and that their wash dissipated quite a bit before you ran into it. Another tough judgement call is an event that occurs on the course to only one crew. What if a wave does hit only your boat? How big must it be to cause a legitimate fairness problem? Even if it was big, what if you were in last place over 30 seconds behind the first place crew? Does it really matter then how big the wave was? Referees are faced with the sometimes unpleasant, yet important task of deciding what's right and what's wrong. When the final decision is made, accept it even though you may not agree with it. Don't act like a major league ballplayer who is upset at a strike call when he feels it was really a ball. Referees position themselves in a place to make the best call - in baseball behind the plate, and in rowing behind the crews in a launch.

Trading shirts is a tradition in some leagues. The winner decides when to make the switch, except when the weather is so bad that rowing back to shore without shirts is a safety risk. If there was a multiple boat race, or all boats land and launch from the same docks, the exchange should occur on shore. If you have to row to a different dock which is rather far away, make the exchange on water. The shirt exchange should be for the

After A Race

shirts raced in, not something else. If the team wore expensive embroidered t-shirts, then everyone should be prepared to lose them. All teams do not share this philosophy, partially due to the cost of the uniforms. Make it clear <u>before the race</u> what shirts you are betting for to avoid any problems later.

PACKING UP FOR THE TRIP HOME

If you win, plan to experience one of the older traditions of rowing - the coxswain toss. The comments you overheard earlier about distance and hang time did not refer to basketball, but to how far you will fly as the oarsmen toss you in. Take off as many clothes as quickly as possible so they don't get wet. Don't forget to leave your wallet if for some reason you brought it along. If the water is really dirty, suggest that your oarsmen throw you in at another place although this suggestion will probably be ignored.

Use the same procedures for packing up for a race listed in Chapter Thirteen, Before A Race to pack up your boat for the trip home. Assign oarsmen to specific tasks. Take charge so there are no surprises when the boat is put back together. Since races occur in poor weather, you may find yourself in the unenviable position of attempting to keep eight tired oarsmen together to quickly and thoroughly take the boat apart while snow, rain, and/or wind blow around you. Get the job done quickly, but carefully so that the first few days of practice after the race are not ruined by half of the boat being out sick or a forgotten part being mailed to you.

AFTER A LOSS

The mental letdown after losing can be a bigger challenge to overcome than the actual problem that caused it. Feelings of losing can demoralize a crew if they are not dealt with properly. If shirts were bet and then lost, rowing to the dock without shirts in front of friends watching on shore is very embarrassing. You should immediately begin to dispel these feelings of failure. During the days after the race, the loss should not be used as a threat, *If we don't get any better than this, we will lose again.* Instead, remind the team of the need to improve, *We need to be faster off the line next time. So let's get those hands away from the body quickly.*

Individual oarsmen who are having a tough time handling the defeat may need specific encouragement. If an oarsman was responsible for the loss by catching a crab, jumping a slide, etc..., there is little you can say to make him feel better. *It happens to the best of them* is not a great line, but it shows the oarsman that you are not holding anything against him. Oarsmen who are upset at losing, but were not individually responsible for it should be dealt with more bluntly, *We tried our best and couldn't do it last Saturday. So let's get our heads up and move on.* If a new strategy is needed, the coach decides this in consultation with the oarsmen. If the high forty at the start of the race that seemed to be a great idea turned out to be a disaster, you may want to only row a high twenty or thirty. If there was extra energy leftover, sprint earlier next time.

AFTER A VICTORY

Rebounding from a victory can be tougher than from a defeat. The pressure to row as correctly as possible due to an upcoming race may no longer be there as some oarsmen begin to feel that they are invincible. Build on the team's experiences in the past race. If the start of the race was spectacular, use that as a goal for the other parts of the race, *We flew off the line last time, but we need to work on the settle so we can continue to cruise down the course.* If the race was a total blowout of your opponent(s), but still demonstrated weaknesses in your boat, honestly state this. Sometimes the best time for bad news is when everyone feels good.

Preparation for a race begins with the response to the previous race(s). Deal with any problems and concerns immediately. The basis for the next race should be the strengths from the previous one. The weaknesses of the past race should be dealt with, not dwelt upon. You should be concerned about the past since you can say something to prevent it. If the boat's slide ratio fell apart at the 800 meter mark in the last race, you could call a *slide ratio twenty* at the 750 meter mark in the next race to focus on and possibly prevent it.

Chapter Seventeen

Seat Racing

• Throughout this chapter, the oarsmen that are racing are <u>underlined</u>. •

Since ergometer scores can only determine an oarsman's physical strength, not his effectiveness, seat racing is often used to determine who moves the boat the fastest. In school programs, most seat racing occurs in February or March. Coaches place a great emphasis upon the results of a seat race to determine the various lineups although other factors do play a part in a coach's decision such as the ability to show up on time for practice, dedication to the team, and an ability to get along with teammates. Someone who can move the boat extremely fast is of little use the day he sleeps in and misses practice, or worse, the bus to the race.

SEAT RACING BASICS

Seat racing involves switching oarsmen between boats after racing them and measuring the change in outcome. If two oarsmen race in different boats and are then switched and no change occurs in the results, both oarsmen are equal in ability. If a change occurs in the results, then one oarsman is better than the other. Seat racing typically takes place in fours, rather than in eights due to the ease of racing smaller boats; the fact that any the change of one oarsman, positive or negative, will be greater in a four than in an eight; the shorter distance a four covers in a set time limit; and the ability to seat race with only eight oarsmen. Not all seat races are obvious to keep everyone guessing so that they have to perform their best in every race. If all eight oarsmen in a seat race in fours raced individually against everyone else on their side, it would take at least sixteen races and most oarsmen would be close to exhaustion by then. A method called **back door** seat racing reduces the number of seat races required.

Assume the following lineup in two standard port rigged boats, Red and Blue, and the oarsmen have the exciting names A, B, C, D, E, F, G, and H. The two boats race twice and the results are shown below in Fugure 17.1. The difference of 1 seat in Race #1 could be due to a slower oarsman, a poorer coxswain, a weight differential, or a combination of these. Don't forget that always winning the first race is not important, since you may lose every other race after that. Since the variables such as wind, current, and your steering should not change between the races, the reason for the different result in Race #2 is that A is now in Blue and E is in Red. Red should have won by one seat if A and E were equal in ability. Red not only lost its 1 seat advantage from the first race, but it also lost by an additional seat. This difference of two seats is how much better A is than E. Thus A won his seat race over E by 2 seats.

In general if the same boat wins both seat races, subtract the results to determine the result. The person in the race with the biggest amount of victory is the winner by that amount. If each boat wins one race, add the difference to determine the result. The oarsman who was always in

Seat Race #1		Seat Race #2	
<u>Red</u>	<u>Blue</u>	<u>Red</u>	<u>Blue</u>
A	E	<u>E</u>	<u>A</u>
B	F	B	F
C	G	C	G
D	H	D	H
Cox 1	Cox 2	Cox 1	Cox 2
Red wins by 1 seat		Blue wins by 1 seat	

Result: A beats E by 2 seats. (1 seat + 1 seat = 2 seats)

Figure 17.1 A sample seat race between A and E.

the winning boat is the winner by that amount.

At all times now or later in the day under the same water conditions, if the coach were to switch back to the original lineup, the results of Race #1 should be duplicated - Red over Blue by 1 seat. This is somewhat like double-checking your work on a math test. Reasons for this not to be true include an oarsman who is only good for a few races, an oarsman who thought that he was done racing for the day and eased up, a poor steering job during one race, etc... Oarsmen are typically lined up against the person they will initially race against, two-man vs. two-man and so on. The boats will use the same lanes in every race. If seat races are done in both directions, the people who are being seat raced should race so that the races that count are in the same direction. This will factor out any change in wind or current.

When discussing results of seat racing, either lengths or seats are used as the standard of measurement. Seats are most accurate - a seat is the space taken up by one oarsman in a boat. Depending upon the hull length, a four is usually considered to be ten seats long- four for the oarsmen, one for the coxswain, and five for the bow and stern decks. An eight is usually considered to be fourteen seats in length. During seat racing, coaches usually find it easier to judge the exact difference won or lost by placing strips of tape on the decks at each point of measurement in case the bowball of one boat finishes the race next to the deck of the other.

Coxswains and oarsmen should learn that the combination of sheer strength and technical abilities determine what is known as the effective force of an oarsman. A 220 pound oarsman exerting the same pressure upon the blade as a 180 pound oarsman will move the boat slower due to the 40 pound difference in weight. The heavier oarsman's effective force is less due to this weight difference. A similar situation is seen when an oarsman with a lower technical ability is matched against another oarsman of the same weight and strength. In this instance, the outcome of a seat race between the two will go to whoever has the greater technical abilities. The athlete who washes out at the finish, is out of time at the catch, or causes the boat to be off set will reduce his effective force and lose his seat race. The term "hammer" is commonly used to refer to someone who has the best ergometer scores in the boathouse, but poor technical abilities. "Hammers" often lose seat races to others who are smaller and a lot slower on the ergometer. Inevitably the "hammers" get frustrated quickly since the off-the-water practices rank them in the top level, but they end up in slower boats when back on the water. Watching a "hammer" in a seat race against a lighter, more efficient oarsman is similar to a David and Goliath struggle. The little guy wins by being smarter and quicker.

THE COACH'S ROLE

Your coach always has the final say in determining the lineup even after seat racing. That's his job. Nevertheless, he listens to a lot of input from oarsmen and coxswains whether asked for or not. A coxswain can have a greater role in seat racing than just handling the boat. Most coaches want input from their coxswains as to the "feel" of the boat when a particular oarsman was in the boat. How was the rhythm or the set? Did the boat feel sluggish at the catch or did it accelerate out of the water? Was the set on starboard and why was that the case? Did someone lean too much one way or have too much wash at the finish? These questions might explain why someone lost his seat race that day even though he seemed much stronger on an ergometer.

Coaches often have a preliminary lineup in mind for the racing season before beginning seat racing. Coaches do this because it makes setting practice lineups easier and represents a best guess by the coach as to who moves the boat the fastest. Coaches generally like to see their beliefs vindicated by seat racing. After all, wouldn't you like your best guess to be correct. However, coaches want the fastest boat to win, not the one that they thought to be the fastest. An unexpected showing by an athlete who moves boats faster than previously thought is a welcome surprise for most coaches. Only a few coaches believe that their previous beliefs were absolutely correct. If this were the case, they would not be seat racing since it would just increase the risk that they would be proved wrong. You should also feel the same way. If an oarsman who you felt did not move the boat well suddenly beats everyone in a seat race, do a better job next time of determining who does.

Chapter Seventeen

Seat Race #1		Seat Race #2		Seat Race #3		Seat Race #4	
Red	Blue	Red	Blue	Red	Blue	Red	Blue
A	E	**E**	**A**	E	A	E	A
B	F	B	F	**F**	**B**	F	B
C	G	C	G	C	G	**G**	**C**
D	H	D	H	D	H	D	H
Cox 1	Cox 2	Cox 1	Cox 2	Cox 1	Cox 2	Cox 1	Cox 2
Red wins by 1 seat		Blue wins by 1 seat		Red wins by 10 seats		Red wins by 3 seats	

A beats E by 2 seats   F beats B by 11 seats   C beats G by 7 seats
(1 seat + 1 seat=2 seats) (10 seats + 1 seat=11 seats)(10 seats - 3 seats=7 seats)
Compare to Race #1   Compare to Race #2   Compare to Race #3

H beats D by 2 seats
(3 seats - 1 seat = 2 seats)
Compare to Race #1

A SAMPLE SEAT RACE DAY

Assume two boats race eight times against each other and the results are listed above. Races #1 and #2 are the same as those listed on the first page of this chapter.

Race #1
This race is the main comparison race. Since everyone knows that the first race could be their seat race and no one is tired, Race #1 is typically the fastest over a set distance.

Race #2
Red had an advantage of 1 seat in Race #1, but has lost by 1 seat. A beats E by 2 seats (1 seat + 1 seat = 2 seats).

Race #3
Blue had an advantage of 1 seat in Race #2, but has lost an additional 10 seats, B looses his seat race by 11 seats (10 seats + 1 seat). This race cannot be compared to race #1 because there two changes have been made since the first race.

Race #4
Blue had an advantage of 10 seats, but now has only a 3 seat advantage. C moves boats 7 seats faster than G. (10 seats - 3 seats)

In Race #4, there was also another seat race that may not be immediately obvious. If only one person was switched, then how can there have been two seat races? Remember that the number of people switched is not important, the actual lineups are. Compare this race lineup to Race #1. Only the coxswains and the strokemen are in the same boats they started in. Thus the strokemen were also seat racing in Race #4 when compared to Race #1. This type of seat race is called a back door seat race since there was not a direct race between the two in consecutive races, such as switching D and H directly. As a result of this race, D has won his race over H by 2 seats. (3 seats - 1 seat = 2 seats) A coach could have brought the boats together and switched all four oarsmen. The lineup would have essentially been the same.

Seat Racing

Seat Race #5		Seat Race #6		Seat Race #7		Seat Race #8	
Red	Blue	Red	Blue	Red	Blue	Red	Blue
E	**G**	**C**	A	C	A	C	A
F	B	F	B	**H**	B	H	**D**
A	C	**G**	**E**	G	E	G	E
D	H	D	H	D	**F**	**B**	F
Cox 1	Cox 2	Cox 1	Cox 2	Cox 1	Cox 2	Cox 1	Cox 2
Red wins by 8 seats		Red wins by 7 seats		Blue wins by 1 seat		Blue wins by 5 seats	
A beats G by 5 seats		E beats G by 3 seats		F beats H by 8 seats		B beats D by 4 seats	
(8 seats - 3 seats=5 seats)		(7 seats - 4 seats=3 seats)		(7 seats + 1 seat=8 seats)		(5 seats - 1 seat=4 seats)	
Compare to Race #4		Compare to Race #3		Compare to Race #6		Compare to Race #7	
C beats A by 2 seats		C beats E by 4 seats					
(10 seats - 8 seats=2 seats)		(7 seats - 3 seats=4 seats)					
Compare to Race #3		Compare to Race #4					

Since coaches typically see the coxswains as part of the equipment during seat racing, thus irrelevant to the outcome (some see you as always irrelevant), the fact that the coxswains did not change would have no bearing on the outcome. If the coxswains are of vastly different skills, one could make the point that this might have had some bearing upon the seat race since D or H may have had a poor warmup from a lousy coxswain which caused Race #1 to be poor and then had to listen to him every race.

Each oarsman has now had a chance to seat race once - three directly and one indirectly. It might seem that any further seat racing would only double-check the initial results. Some coaches will do so and some won't, depending upon the availability of time and how close the seat races were. As mentioned before, seat racing accuracy depends on the type of boat and the length of the race. Since F beat B by 11 seats and C beat G by 7 seats, there is little chance, if any, of a markedly different outcome with a re-row. In the case of A and E in Race #2, the outcome is so close, 2 seats, that a re-race would probably be of some help to the coach to test endurance. He might also seat race these two oarsmen in bigger boats (eights rather than fours) and in a longer race (four or five minutes versus three minutes).

Race #5
Red had an advantage of 3 seats in Race #4 and then wins by 8 sets in Race #5. Compared to Race #4, A beats G by 5 seats (8 seats - 3 seats). Compared to Race #3, C beats A by 2 seats (10 seats - 8 seats).

Race #6
Red had an advantage of 8 seats in Race #5, but then wins by only 7 seats. Compared to Race #3, E beats G by 3 seats (7 seats - 4 seats). Compared to Race #4, C beats E by 4 seats (7 seats - 3 seats).

Race #7
Red had an advantage of 7 seats in Race #6, but then looses by 1 seat. Compared to Race #6, F beats H by 8 seats (7 seats + 1 seat).

Race #8
Blue had an advantage of 1 seat in Race #7, then wins by 5 seats. Compared to Race #7, B beats D by 4 seats (5 seats - 1 seat).

Chapter Seventeen

The final result of these seat races have determined a ranking of the oarsmen. From highest to lowest order, the rank on port side is C by 2 seats over A by 2 seats over E by 3 seats over G. On starboard side the rank is F by 7 seats over D by 1 seat over H by 3 seats over B. Thus F beats B by 11 seats (7+1+3 = 11).

Note that these races could have been held in any order. The order listed above was done solely to make it easier to see who was being raced. Since some coaches may not like their oarsmen to know who is being seat raced, they may purposely mix up the races. Since results of seat races slightly vary from race to race even with the same lineups, do not assume that a victory of one seat in a four is a major victory. If only D and H had previously rowed in the stroke seat, F and B would be at a disadvantage when they row in the stroke seat. However since they both had to do it, and their seat races were consecutive this is not a concern. However, if these two had been switched far apart such as F in Race #2 and B in Race #7 the seat race would not be totally fair. These results are based upon racing in conditions that do not change throughout the course of the day. This is another reason that coaches generally like to compare two consecutive races, rather than two far apart

THE COXSWAIN'S ROLE

Your role in a seat race is to ensure that every oarsman faces the same conditions as everyone else, just like ergometer testing. The warmup for seat racing should be very similar to a warmup for a race although there should be a greater emphasis upon the maximum strokerate set by your coach that cannot be exceeded during the seat racing. Seat racing requires you to keep a perfectly straight course each race, display the same aggressiveness, and favor no one in the actions you take. Most seat races have a maximum strokerate. It is your job during a seat race to let your strokeman and the whole boat know what the strokerate is and if you need to lower it. There will be very few times that you will need to raise the strokerate in a seat race - no one wants to give the other boat an advantage. Though you are racing against another boat, act, talk, and think that you are racing against another team with the same restrictions upon what you say as for ergometer testing listed in Chapter Twelve, On Land Workouts.

The seat race should start as evenly as possible. The goal is for the boats to match each other exactly in strokerate, pressure, and catch timing. One boat should be designated as the leader and one and the follower. Most coaches begin seat races by having the boats stop side by side and then starting the boats together. Some coaches with experienced coxswains in both boats will allow the coxswains to bring their boats alongside each other and then give the starting commands. If for some reason the boats do not begin the seat race even, this difference will be subtracted out of the results. However, anything greater than a difference of two seats will be an unfair advantage for the leading boat.

SWITCHING OARSMEN BETWEEN BOATS

There are two methods of switching oarsmen between boats. The first method is for the coach to ferry the oarsmen between the boats in his launch. This requires very little skill on your part. The second method requires that the oarsmen switch themselves directly. One coxswain stops his boat several lengths ahead of the other boat. The other coxswain brings his boat in at a 15 degree angle, similar to a landing, but very slowly. Row the boats together so that the blade of your bowman or two-man will just touch the other boat near the bowman or two-man. The oarsmen can then grab onto the other boat's blades to pull the boats together so that the bowmen are next to each other and so on. Never use this method in rough weather or strong currents since you have very little control of your boat when they are pulled together.

As the boats are being pulled together, both boats must lean away from each other to prevent the riggers from resting on and damaging the hulls. After the boats are pulled together, keep the boats tilted away from each other; otherwise kiss your gunwales good-bye although most oarsmen will be too tired to care or pay attention. When the boats are lined up beside each other, oarsmen can switch individually or simultaneously. Having five oarsmen in one boat for a few seconds will not damage or sink it. Your ability to control your boat's

Seat Racing

course will be limited so switch oarsmen far away from any obstructions that you might drift into. When the oarsmen are switched, both boats should lean away, push off, and tie in. After a short bit of rowing together, call a race pace ten to warmup the boat and give you an indication what you can expect during the seat race.

Seat racing is not a perfect tool for determining boat lineups. But a fair seat race is about as close as one can get. You must be as fair as possible in the actions you take during seat racing. Unfortunately for coxswains, seat races are not helpful for determining who is the better coxswain for a boat. Sometimes the best judgement of who is the better coxswain is by a vote of the oarsmen in that boat. At least you will not have to run yourself into the ground like the oarsmen do in seat races.

Chapter Eighteen

Basic Rigging

Rigging is one of the most misunderstood topics of rowing. It unfairly gets the blame when something goes wrong, but may be unnoticed when something does. Rigging has an almost mystical image to many who feel that there are "secrets" in it which can be unleashed only after several years of experience. This perception is an incorrect one. Rigging can be complicated because it does cover a range of factors that all interact with each other. But just like the confusion surrounding seat racing, the "mysteries" of rigging can be mastered by anyone who takes the time to learn them. Since whole books have been written about rigging, this chapter does not attempt to explain everything there is to be known about rigging. Instead, this chapter briefly explains what you as a coxswain need to know. Your coach will adjust the rigging on your boat, although it helps for you to understand the dynamics of rigging when you mention a possible problem to him.

RIGGING FUNDAMENTALS

Rigging generally deals with positions of the blade and oarsmen within the boat. These positions interact with each other and make it difficult to find easy solutions to large problems. Adjusting one setting will usually impact upon the settings of other parts. Trial and error is a large part of the rigging process. The major areas of rigging are:

1. The pitch of the oarlocks
2. The actual measurements of the rigger - **spread**, **outboard**, **inboard**, etc...
3. The position of the shoes in the boat (How far/close are they to the stern)
4. The angle of the shoes on the footboards

Figure 18.1 A quick fix to rigging which is too high - a seat pad.

Basic Rigging

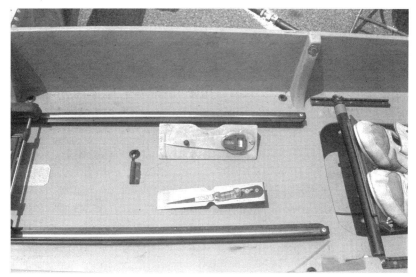

Figure 18.2 Two pitchmeters lying on the strokeman's seat next to the strokerate sensor.

Figure 18.3 A rigger stick to support the boat while checking the rigging.

0 1 2 3 4 5 6 7 8
Angles of pitch while looking sideways at a port blade.

← **Figures 18.4 and 18.5** What pitch looks like. →

8 7 6 5 4 3 2 1 0
Angles of pitch while looking sideways at a starboard blade.

111

Chapter Eighteen

The basic terms of rigging are:

Pitch — The measurement of an angle. In general use, pitch refers to the vertical angle of the blade when the oar sits in the oarlock. Pitch can also refer to the angle of the footboards and to the outward angle of an oarlock. Pitch is changed by adjusting the pin or the plastic pitch inserts. See Chapter Two, Equipment.

Height/Depth — The height of the oar handle varies with the depth of the blade - a higher oar means more depth, a lower oar means less depth. A short oarsman rowing in a seat rigged for a tall oarsman will wash out. A tall oarsman rowing in a set rigged for a short oarsman will dig the blade. Height is adjusted by lowering or rasing the pin. A temporary fix is to use a set pad. (see **Figure 18.1**)

Load — How much resistance an oarsman feels on his oar. If a load is too heavy, the oarsman will not be able to keep up and will become exhausted early. If a load is too light, the oarsman will be early at the finish and not be able to use all of his power to move the boat. The load is somewhat equivalent to a gear in a car or bike. Load is adjusted by moving either the collar on the oar or the rigger outwards or inwards.

Inboard — The distance from the end of the oar handle to the edge of the collar. The greater the inboard, the less distance the oar is extended into the water, thereby reducing the amount of load. Inboard is adjusted by changing the collar or spread.

Outboard — The distance from the end of the blade and the edge of the collar. The greater the outboard, the more the oar is extended into the water, thereby increasing the load on the blade. Outboard is adjusted by changing the collar or spread.

Spread — The distance between the oarlocks. This number is related to inboard. Maintaining all other settings, the greater the spread, the greater the inboard. Spread is adjusted by changing the rigging.

BLADE PITCH

The most noticeable part of rigging for oarsmen and coxswains is the pitch of the blade. A blade with too much pitch will dig into the water; a blade with too little pitch will wash out. Pitch also keeps the leading edge of the blade higher than the trailing edge of the blade on the recovery so that the blade will not be caught by a wave. Blades should always have some pitch to help keep them buried through the stroke and to prevent the blade from being caught by a wave on the recovery. Pitch is a matter of personal preference for oarsmen, but the general range is from 4 to 7 degrees.

Pitch can be adjusted temporarily on the water by wrapping black tape around either the top or bottom of the oarlock - not the middle. Wrapping tape around the top will reduce the amount of pitch; wrapping it around the bottom will increase it. If your three-man frequently washes out, black tape on the bottom of the oarlock may help. He may also have difficulty rowing because he is rigged too high. A butt pad or shim on the top bolt of the mainstay between the rigger and the hull would lower the height of the rigger.

Outward pitch is more complicated to understand. Outward pitch adjusts the amount of regular pitch as the oar swings through the stroke. If you were to look at the oarlock from the side while it points from bow to stern, outward pitch would result in a lean of the oarlock towards you. This measurement is not important enough for a coxswain to worry about until he is coxing an elite boat.

BLADE HEIGHT/DEPTH

A six foot six oarsman will not be able to row with the same rigging as a five foot six oarsman. If the boat was properly rigged for the taller oarsman, the shorter oarsmen will need to keep his hands way up in the air

Basic Rigging

to keep the blade buried. This makes the blade difficult to control and will likely result in the shorter oarsman being unable to bury the blade properly and having too high of a blade height off the water on the recovery. A **shim** between the top mainstay bar and the hull will temporarily lower the rigger height, and a shim between the bottom bar of the mainstay and the hull will raise it. Too many shims will make rowing difficult because the outward pitch will be too great.

BLADE LOAD

The outboard and inboard measurements determine how much leverage is applied to the oar. An oar with too little load will be pulled through the water too quickly with minimal propulsion of the boat. Too much load will make it difficult for an oarsman to row through the water quickly enough to maintain high racing strokerates. Load is adjustable by changing either the settings of the collar and/or the oarlock pin. An oarsman who seems to be the **hammer** in the boat will out-pull his weaker teammates. To use more of his power, the load should be increased on his blade. The visible result of this change will be that the tip of the blade sticks out from the rest of the blade tips on the recovery when viewed from behind the stern.

FOOT STRETCHER SETTINGS

The foot stretchers are the base from which oarsmen push off for the drive. The distance the foot stretchers are from the end of the slide and the angle of the footboards control the distance oarsmen row through the water as well as their ability to row comfortably. Most coaches prefer novices to set their foot stretchers so that the rear wheels almost touch the back stops of the slide at the finish. Other coaches prefer to set the stretchers a certain distance from the front stops of the slide at the catch. Either ensures that all blades are equally spaced at one point of the stroke - the catch or the finish. What is often assumed about the tracks of the slide is that they are fixed in position. This is not true since the slide tracks are adjustable and may loosen up over time. They can be loosened or tightened with wingnuts located underneath the tracks. Before basing your decision on where to put the foot stretchers, ensure that each track is the same distance from the foot stretcher parts which are permanently bolted onto the boat.

Another adjustable setting of the foot stretchers is the angle of the footboards which the shoes rest on. The footboard angle is a matter of personal comfort, although an angle which varies tremendously from the usual may prevent an oarsman from fully compressing. If an oarsman seems unable to pull himself forward as much as everyone else on the recovery, have him sit at the catch while next to the dock. His seat may be hitting the tracks or he may be unable to compress further without hurting his ankles due to the footboard angle. A rough visual comparison with everyone else's foot boards will allow you or the coach to judge whether or not the footboards have the proper angle.

Rigging can be complicated if you try to understand too many things at once. Every measurement in rigging is related to other measurements. For this reason, do not assume that a blatant rigging problem can be solved with one adjustment. Changing the height of the rigger may require you to adjust the pitch of the blade as well as the outward pitch. Always ask your coach before you even think about changing the rigging. Though the boat is "yours", the rigging is "his." Since rigging is complicated, expect that it will take a long time to master. It may take several years for you to become an expert at it, although some coxswains never do.

Chapter Nineteen

Conclusion

    Coxswains rarely hop into the varsity boat in their first year. In some large programs, coxswains average up to three years to make it to the lead boat and many never will. Some coxswains gain too much weight, decide coxing isn't for them, or fail miserably at coxing due to either improper instruction or lack of natural skill. The key to winning a seat in the top boat is the same as the key for oarsmen - constant improvement. Your competition is clearer - five or six coxswains compared to fifty oarsmen.
    Coaches sometimes will place coxswains solely by seniority, but most look to pick the best coxswain with only some regard for seniority. If two coxswains that both know every drill, term, and technique are compared, they still may be unequal. See Chapter Thirteen, Before A Race for these reasons. As mentioned in the beginning, this book can only take you so far. A large part of a coxswain's skill after learning the basics is gained purely from experience. Having been there and making mistakes is a large part of the process, but do not look to make mistakes in order to improve. Study mistakes made by others. If after your workout you see a boat having a tough time landing, put yourself in that coxswain's shoes and think what you would do. Watch videos of other boats and think of what drills you would use to improve that boat's performance. As you plan in your mind what rate of improvement your team will make throughout the season, plan your own improvement. Just as increasing physical endurance takes time, so do problems made by oarsmen or coxswains. Practice makes perfect, and you will have lots of practice.

TOUGH TIMES

    There will be days, weeks, or even seasons when everything seems to be going against you. A one-day problem might be an equipment problem combined with your failure to follow the coaches' directions for the workout. Sure, you will feel miserable after a rough day, but the key is to bounce back from adversity. If you cannot come back from being "down" personally, how can you expect to bring a boat back from being "down" two seats in a race.
    Probably the two worst things that can happen to a coxswain is that your hull is damaged by something you ran into/over or you are disqualified from a race because of a steering problem or your lack of following directions. In the situations when you should have known better, you will feel that you are six inches tall and deservedly so. In the situations when the incident may not have been foreseen, put up with the grief, apologize for the incident even if it may not have been your fault, and put it behind you. Most everyone will drop the incident from their memory within a few weeks.

THE YEARS AHEAD

    Increasingly, there will be less to learn, but more to expect from an experienced coxswain. Hopefully, you have mastered what can be read about coxing within three years. Your knowledge will increasingly come from what you can sense or hear within the boat, not just what you see. You will have coxed through a few seasons. Your boats may have had a winning season each of these years, but a combination of winning and

Conclusion

losing seasons will prepare you more for the advanced levels of coxing. Steering will become an instinct. As the boat turns to one side, you will compensate for it without even being aware of your steering. The oarsmen will feel comfortable with your guidance about the proper style. Landings will become a non-event. Your mastery of drills will allow the coach to tell you what he is looking for that day so that you can come up with the drills that will get you there. Hopefully, your coach will use you as more than a megaphone. He may begin to regularly consult with you for your ideas of drills or workouts.

This book has attempted to speed that process up, but cannot eliminate it. Poor coxswains typically reach a plateau of learning and then stagnate, or even grow worse as they become more frustrated. Just as <u>good</u> wines improve with age, so do <u>good</u> coxswains. Your goal is to be a good coxswain that always continues to improve.

As you learn the basics of coxing, you lay the basis for a path where constant improvement continues. Your improvement will not be as great or as visible as it was when you first started. No one has rowed or coxed a perfect race filled with perfect strokes, and no one ever will. There is always room for improvement. You must have this attitude with you as you cox. If you feel that you know all you need to know about rowing and coxing, then you have actually stopped learning and will not proceed any further. Good luck.

<u>Please do not hesitate to share your comments about this book. Please direct them to:</u>
The Coxswain's Locker, Inc.
P.O. Box 1167
Washington, DC 20013
www.coxing.com